Kathleen Ralph

BECOMING A Celestial PERSON IN A TELESTIAL WORLD

BECOMING

Celestial

A PERSON

IN A

TELESTIAL

WORLD

ALLAN K. BURGESS

BOOKCRAFT
Salt Lake City, Utah

Library of Congress Catalog Card Number: 90-82471

ISBN 0-88494-752-1

First Printing, 1990

Printed in the United States of America

Contents

Introduction

Some of us struggle with temptations. Others lack the understanding to endure difficult situations. Many of us desire more help in our family relationships. Most of us yearn to feel closer to God and to better recognize the whisperings of the Spirit. Some of us feel at a loss on how to help friends or family members with problems because we don't know how to approach them, or we feel that we are struggling as much as they are. All of us, from time to time, feel promptings from the Spirit to become better people and live up to the potential we have as children of God.

This telestial world affects each one of us differently. All of the above desires are manifestations of different spiritual needs. Through a better understanding and application of the gospel, and with the help of the Holy Ghost, all of these desires and needs can be better fulfilled.

For over twenty-five years, I have had the pleasure of teaching the gospel to both teenagers and adults. Opportunities have allowed me also to serve in many other rewarding positions in the Church. Most of these opportunities have put me in direct contact with people who were in the process of changing their lives for the better. One of my greatest privileges has been to work with and teach hundreds of couples who were preparing themselves to go to the temple. These experiences have given me the opportunity to see many people start living celestial principles in spite of the telestial forces with which all of us are faced.

Most of us have probably seen people who, with the help of the Lord, have broken out of spiritual and emotional bondage and become worthy sons and daughters of God. As we become involved with those who are changing for the better, we soon come to realize that every one of us has the potential and capacity to live celestial lives because we are literal children of God.

Participating in and observing this growth process has taught me that in order for spiritual growth to occur, a person must understand and apply certain fundamental principles of the gospel. Each chapter in this book discusses one of these important concepts and has been approached with at least three basic goals in mind:

1. To teach with clarity and simplicity a basic gospel principle or doctrine that leads to increased celestial growth

2. To teach *why* that particular principle or doctrine is important to celestial growth and *how* to apply it in this telestial world of ours

3. To include stories and illustrations that are both enlightening and motivating so that the gospel principle can be better understood and applied

This book has been written because of the joy I have felt as I have seen people come to understand gospel principles and receive the happiness that comes through living them. My heart is filled with love for each member of the Church. I know that all of us are brothers and sisters and that we need each other's help in order to fulfill our celestial destiny. My hope is that the ideas and concepts presented in this book will bring to those who read it a greater desire and ability to draw closer to God and develop the attributes that spring from their divine parentage.

1

Three Basic Truths

Many of us underestimate how important we are to our Father in Heaven. Betty and Allan were a couple who felt just this way. They had no idea how much God loved them until they came face to face with a devastating crisis.

Just five weeks after having gone through open-heart surgery, Betty found out she had cancer. When the doctors operated they discovered that the cancer had spread throughout most of her body. Because her heart stopped briefly during the operation, and because the cancer was so widespread, they performed only minor surgery and closed Betty back up.

When the doctors told the couple that Betty had approximately six weeks to live, the news was overwhelming. It was especially difficult for Allan. They had done everything together and were each other's best friends. As Allan tried to absorb the news, a huge feeling of emptiness filled his soul.

Just two weeks later the Lord manifested his great love for Betty and Allan. They were attending the October conference on Temple Square in Salt Lake City, and when the morning session ended they hurried out of the Tabernacle with the hope of being able to get a closer look at President McKay —and possibly even to shake his hand. But for some reason no one was allowed to get close to the prophet that morning.

Slightly disappointed, the couple left Temple Square and began the walk back to their car. As they walked hand in hand down the sidewalk, a car pulled up next to them. It was President McKay's car, and he had asked his driver to stop. The prophet rolled down his window, looked directly at Betty for a moment or two, and quietly said, "I'll see you this afternoon, Sister." He then rolled up the window, and the car drove away.

This incident astonished Betty and Allan, as they had no idea what it meant. They had planned to return to their home and watch the afternoon session of conference on television, but they quickly adjusted their plans and hurried to get in line for the session. Following the meeting they again went around behind the Tabernacle to see what would happen. As they waited quietly, neither of them anticipated the great blessing that was soon going to come into their lives.

As President McKay stepped out of the Tabernacle, his eyes scanned the crowd until they rested on Betty. He then walked directly up to her and lovingly took her by the arm. As he touched her, she felt the power of his great spirit flow from him to her, and tears came to her eyes as the Holy Ghost witnessed to her that he truly was a prophet of God. President McKay guided her away from the crowd and led her between some of the Tabernacle pillars where they could be alone. He then took her by the hand and talked to her for several minutes. He told her things that her soul needed to hear. He told her that God loved her and that she would be all right. He said that she didn't need to worry anymore.

Betty was so filled with the spirit that radiated from this great man that she became physically weak and began to shake. After President McKay left, Allan took her by the hand and helped her sit down on one of the nearby benches. He kept asking her what President McKay had said, but it took her several minutes before she could stop trembling and gain her composure enough to answer him.

The next week, Betty and Allan went to California to visit relatives. The trip had originally been planned so that Betty could say her good-byes, but now they did not know what to think. They were not sure what President McKay had meant when he had told Betty that she would be all right. Because Betty was so weak she had received a beautiful blessing from her stake president before she and her husband left on their trip.

While in California, they participated in baptisms for the dead as well as several temple sessions. During one of these sessions, the Lord reached out and once again showed his great love for Betty and Allan. While they were participating in a prayer, the temple worker offering the prayer said that a woman was present who had traveled a great distance to be there. He mentioned that she had come with her family and had received a blessing from her priesthood leader before coming. A sweet comforting spirit enveloped Betty as she realized he was praying for her. The one praying then proceeded to give Betty the same blessing, almost word for word, as she had received it from her stake president. Tears came to her eyes, and peace and gratitude entered her heart.

This experience was very special for Betty, but it was especially meaningful to Allan. He realized for the first time just how important each one of us is to our Father in Heaven. That day in the temple he came to understand how much God loved both of them, and from that time forth he has desired to reciprocate that love. He still cannot discuss this experience without choking up with emotion and tears coming to his eyes.

When Betty returned to the doctor the following week, all signs of the cancer were gone. She had been totally healed.

This experience helped Betty and Allan, and can help all of us, better understand that the Lord knows each one of us personally. Betty learned that God does not just reveal programs and information for groups but is also concerned for each individual. In Betty's case, at least three priesthood leaders, including the prophet, were inspired in her behalf.

There are three very basic truths that, when understood in our hearts and not just in our minds, can bring a great sense of peace and confidence into all of our lives, just as they did into the lives of Betty and Allan.

Truth number one is that each one of us is literally a spirit child of God. We are the offspring of divine, eternal heavenly parents. This leads to truth number two, which is that, since we are God's children, he knows and loves each one of us personally and individually. The third great truth is that, because of his great love for us, our Heavenly Father will never ask us to do anything that will not be for the benefit of ourselves or of his other children. Everything he asks us to do will eventually bring us peace and happiness.

In the next three chapters we will explore these basic truths and perhaps come to better understand just how valuable and loved we really are. An understanding of these truths is the foundation upon which we can build celestial lives in spite of the telestial environment that surrounds us.

2

Celestial
Parentage

Knowing who we really are is of vital importance to our celestial growth. The story has been told about a salesman who went to an isolated valley on a sales trip. He was planning on spending several days there but found there were no hotels or rooming houses where he could stay. He looked around until he found the finest-looking house in the valley, knocked on the door, and asked the rancher if he could stay the night. The hospitable rancher invited him to come in and make himself at home. The two men had such an enjoyable evening together that the salesman decided to get up early and help his new friend with the chores.

As the salesman was feeding the chickens, much to his surprise he saw an eagle among them. He yelled excitedly to the rancher to warn him about the eagle, but the rancher didn't seem at all concerned and told him not to worry about it. The salesman tried again to warn the rancher and told him how dangerous an eagle could be among chickens, but the rancher was still unconcerned. Finally the rancher said, "Let me tell you a story and then you will understand."

The year before, the rancher had found an eagle's nest on a cliff high up in the mountains. In the nest he had found three eggs. He had taken two of the eggs back to his ranch and put them under a brooding hen. One of the eggs had hatched, and that is how the eagle had gotten there. The eagle thought the hen was his mother and the other chickens were his brothers and sisters. He did not realize he was an eagle but instead thought he was a chicken.

When the salesman looked into the farmyard again, sure enough there was the eagle scratching around in the dirt looking for something to eat along with the chickens. The salesman had always liked a challenge, and he asked the rancher if he would mind his performing an experiment with the eagle. Since the eagle couldn't lay eggs, the rancher indicated that he didn't mind at all.

The salesman walked over to the eagle, picked it up in his hands, and said, "You're an eagle. Take to your wings and fly." The eagle just blinked at him with his big yellow eyes, ruffled up his feathers, and looked him up and down before hopping down to the ground and starting to scratch for grains of corn in the dirt again. The rancher just laughed and said, "See, I told you he was just a chicken." The salesman shook his head. "It just isn't right," he said, and he went out to sell his product.

He spent another pleasant evening with the rancher and again fed the chickens the next morning. Once again he picked up the eagle and told him who and what he was, but the bird still didn't seem to believe him. Instead of flying, the eagle hopped down and started scratching in the dirt again.

On the third day the salesman went out very early in the morning just as the sun was coming up over the mountain. He reached down, lifted up the eagle, and turned him so that he was facing the sun. Then he said again, "You are a golden eagle, take to your wings and fly!" Once again the eagle just looked at him and blinked, but as he did so the sun shone in his eyes. The eagle raised his head and looked up at the light. All of a sudden he began to tremble; then he spread his great wings and off he flew. He never scratched in the dirt with the chickens again. He was no longer a chicken but a golden eagle, the king of the birds. When he started looking up instead of down he finally realized who and what he was. (See Theodore M. Burton, in Conference Report, April 1962, pp. 55-57.)

In the Old Testament, when David had considered the majesty and breadth of the stars in the heavens, he asked God: "What is man, that thou art mindful of him? and the son of man, that thou visitest him?" (Psalm 8:4.)

The answer to this question was beautifully given by President J. Reuben Clark, Jr., when he said, "Man is greater and grander, more precious according to the arithmetic of God, than all of the planets and suns of space. For man were they created. They are the handiwork of God. . . . Man is his son." (From LDS film *This Is My Glory.*)

Yes, we are the children of God, and as we come to understand this simple, profound truth it will bring us a feeling of self-worth and dignity that can come to us in no other way. Elder Boyd K. Packer asked, "What could inspire one to purity and worthiness more than to possess a spiritual confirmation that we are the children of God? What could inspire a more lofty regard for oneself, or engender more love for mankind? This thought does not fill me with arrogance. It fills me with overwhelming humility." (*Ensign,* November 1984, p. 68.)

As we consider the pattern of the world around us we realize that puppies always grow up to be dogs and kittens always mature to become cats. No puppies become cats and no kittens become dogs. All animals inherit a certain genetic pattern that allows them to become like their parents. With this in mind, what a reverent and awe-inspiring thought it is to realize we are the children of God. Each one of us is of the family of the gods and has inherited the "celestial genes" necessary to become like our divine and eternal heavenly parents.

Once this important truth is truly understood, we will never be the same again. Just as the eagle did, we can look up and make the decision to fulfill our destiny. Because of our divine parentage and the atonement of Christ, we can become more godlike here and achieve godhood in the world to come. Some people say, "But I'm just not a religious person." This of course is not true. We lived with our heavenly parents for many more years than we have lived here upon the earth, and all indications show that during that period of time we were very religious. We fought on the Savior's side in the premortal existence for the opportunity of coming to this earth so we could eventually become like our heavenly parents. Like the eagle, some of us have temporarily forgotten who we really are.

Sometimes we fall into the trap of comparing ourselves with others. This may be because the world we live in has become so competitive. For many, winning at all costs seems to have become their major goal. God, however, works on a different level of intelligence. He has established a beautiful plan that allows all of us to be winners if that is what we truly desire.

The following story about winning is instructive. While a young boy was helping his father in the garden, he asked his dad if he could come and watch him run in a race at school on the following Friday. When the dad said that he could be there, the son was very excited. The son then said, "I won't win the race, Dad, but I want you to come anyway." The boy was quiet for a minute or two and then said, "Dad, I'll probably come in last. I can't run very fast, but I still want you to come and watch me run."

Friday came, and the boy was even more excited. He got up in the morning and said, "This is it! This is the big day we have been waiting for."

On the way to the school the boy said, "Dad, you know even if I come in last, I'm still going to get a prize. Our teacher told us she didn't think it was fair that only winners should get a prize."

When they arrived at the school, the dad sat in the bleachers with the other parents while the children played several games. Finally it was time for the big first grade race. As the boys positioned themselves at the starting line, the boy looked up at his father as if to say, "Dad, this is it. This is the great race you came to watch."

The teacher blew her whistle and the boys were off. The father watched as his boy ran as hard as he could. He watched the legs of his little boy move as fast as he could move them, mostly up and down rather than forward. When the boy was about ten feet away from the finish line, he couldn't restrain himself any longer; he had to turn his head around and see if his dad was still looking. As he did so he stumbled and fell. The rest of the boys crossed the finish line ahead of him. The father watched as his son crawled across the goal line on his hands and knees. He saw the teacher reach down, take hold of his hand, and lift him up. The father saw a smile blossom across the face of his son as the teacher handed him his prize, an all-day sucker. As the boy reached the bleachers he looked at his dad and said, "Dad, did you see me run?" (See Ray F. Smith, *Prison Work—You Can't Judge a Man by His Record*, Brigham Young University Speeches of the Year [Provo, 5 February 1957].)

We are not involved in a race or any other type of competition with our brothers and sisters here upon the earth. We are here to do the best we can do. When we fall down, God will help us get up again, and it doesn't matter if those around us seem to be running better or faster. There is a prize beyond comprehension for all those who finish. We can all become celestial people if we will use and develop the abilities and characteristics that we have inherited from our celestial parents.

3

Individual
Worth

Have you ever found yourself pondering about the millions of people here upon this earth and wondering if God really knows you personally and is concerned with your individual welfare? Perhaps you have gazed into the heavens on a clear night and been overwhelmed by the vastness of the universe and the myriad stars. You may have questioned how a creator of such power and scope could be aware of and concerned with just one person.

As we contemplate the ability of God to know each of us personally, it might help us to consider the world around us. Man has invented electronic equipment that makes it possible to see or hear someone from anywhere in the world. Millions of pieces of information about people can be retrieved with the push of a button. Men and equipment can be transported to the moon and even further into space, and still stay in communication with the earth. If man with his limited intelligence and knowledge can produce such mind-boggling accomplishments, is it difficult to believe that God, who is the Creator and Father of us all, can listen to and communicate with us? The important thing, however, is not how God keeps track of each one of us; rather, it is that he does. Because we are his children, not only as a group but also as individuals, he is mindful and personally interested in every one of us.

The scriptures tell us that God loves us and is concerned for our welfare. He has told us that he spends his time and effort helping us gain immortality and eternal life (see Moses 1:39). He watches over each man, woman, and child just as an earthly father watches over his children. Jesus taught that not even one sparrow is forgotten by God and that even the very hairs of our heads are numbered. He taught that we do not need to fear that we are not known to God, because each one of us is of more value than many sparrows. (See Luke 12:6-7.)

Joseph Millett was a member of the Church in the 1800s. He had a large family, and, at a time in his life when he was going through difficult times, he discovered that God knew him personally. He recorded the following experience in his journal:

One of my children came in, said that Brother Newton Hall's folks were out of bread. Had none that day. I put . . . our flour in sack to send up to Brother Hall's. Just then Brother Hall came in. Says I, "Brother Hall, how are you out for flour." "Brother Millett, we have none." "Well, Brother Hall, there is some in that sack. I have divided and was going to send it to you. Your children told mine that you were out." Brother Hall began to cry. Said he had tried others. Could not get any. Went to the cedars and prayed to the Lord and the Lord told him to go to Joseph Millett. "Well, Brother Hall, you needn't bring this back if the Lord sent you for it. You don't owe me for it." You can't tell how good it made me feel to know that the Lord knew that there was such a person as Joseph Millett. (As quoted in Eugene England, *Why the Church Is As True As the Gospel* [Salt Lake City: Bookcraft, 1986], p. 30.)

Brother Hall also learned that day that God knew him personally as he was directed to a home where he could receive help. God knows and loves each of us personally. He is aware of our needs and our wants, our problems and our successes, our highs and our lows. Whether we make good choices or bad choices, his love never wavers.

President Benson taught that "God loves us. He's watching us, he wants us to succeed, and we'll know someday that he has not left one thing undone for the eternal welfare of each of us. If we only knew it, there are heavenly hosts pulling for us—friends in heaven that we can't remember now, who yearn for our victory. This is our day to show what we can do." (*Ensign*, July 1975, p. 63.)

If we reflect upon our lives we will realize that the Lord has shown his great love for us numerous times and in many different, and sometimes unusual, ways. The following account, related by Elder Glen L. Rudd of the First Quorum of the Seventy, represents the kind of experience to which many can testify.

Flavia Salazar Gomez grew up in Mexico. She was baptized when she was twelve years old along with her mother and sisters. As she reached maturity, she fell in love with and married a man from the Dominican Republic. She moved with him back to his country, where she thought that she was the only Church member in the country of five million people.

One day she wrote a letter, in Spanish, to Glen Rudd, who was then serving as president of the Florida Mission. She told him she had a year-old baby who had not received a name or a blessing from a priesthood holder. She explained that she was seriously ill with cancer and had been told by the doctors that she would not live much longer. She wondered if someone who held the priesthood could come to her city and give the baby and her a blessing.

President Rudd wrote back and told her he would visit her as soon as he possibly could. A short time later he was asked to attend a conference in Puerto Rico. He only knew of one family that lived in the general area where Flavia lived, the

Dale Valentine family. They lived in a city about ninety miles away from where Flavia lived. He wrote Brother Valentine and asked him if he would meet him at the airport and take him to see Flavia.

As President Rudd's party arrived at the outskirts of Flavia's city after several hours of strenuous driving, they realized that they did not know where Flavia lived. They had no street address of any kind but had only her name.

They stopped for a few minutes on a high hill overlooking the city, and then President Rudd told them to drive into the city and turn left, which they did. Then he told them to make a right turn and proceed toward the center of this very large city. After doing so, they drove for several blocks looking for a parking place but couldn't find one. After driving for several more blocks they felt prompted to go to the next corner and make a right turn, and before they knew it they had found an empty parking space. They parked the car, and Brother Valentine said, "Now what do we do?" President Rudd said, "Let's just start asking people."

They saw a man leaning up against the front of a home and asked him, in Spanish, if he knew Flavia Salazar Gomez. The man was surprised and said, "Yes, she's my wife. She's just inside that door."

Before they gave her a blessing, Brother Valentine interviewed Flavia to see how close she had stayed to the teachings of the Church. It had been over two years since she had left Mexico and had had contact with the Church in any way. They were happy to find that she was living the Word of Wisdom and praying every day. She was doing her best to be a good, faithful member.

They named and blessed her little boy and then gave Flavia a beautiful blessing. They were inspired to bless her that she would be healed from her cancerous condition. When they checked with her about six months later, she was healthy and happy, and the cancer was gone.

The Lord knew Flavia personally, and he knew the men who were directed to her doorstep. (See *Ensign*, January 1989, pp. 71–72.)

When our Heavenly Father sent us down to this earth to work out our exaltation, he did not leave us alone. He gave us the Savior and his great atonement so that we could have the chance to return to him. He gave us the scriptures to guide and help us to make correct decisions throughout our lives. We have living prophets and Apostles to help us better understand the scriptures and help us apply the word of God as we face today's problems and challenges. We also have the gift of the Holy Ghost, which brings us great comfort, peace, and guidance as we strive to do the will of our Father. One of the greatest gifts that he has given us is the opportunity to communicate with him each day in holy and sacred prayer. He has told us that we can pray to him silently as well as vocally, and discuss with him our temporal, as well as our spiritual and emotional, needs.

Because we are his children our Heavenly Father loves each one of us and desires to help each of us become as he is. The realization that we are loved of God is the very basis of our relationship with him. As this truth sinks deep within our hearts, we develop the faith and confidence in God that we need in order to place our lives in his hands.

4

The Better Way

The story is told of an old fox-hunter who had been very successful. When he grew older he decided to retire and move south during the winters. As he was preparing to close up his hunting area he was approached by a young man who wanted to become a successful fox-hunter. This young man offered to pay the older man well if he would sell him his shop and hunting area and teach him the secrets that had made him so successful.

The old hunter agreed and carefully taught the youngster all the skills and secrets that would lead to success. The old man then went south for the winter season, leaving the young man well trained and qualified to carry on in his place.

When the winter was over, the old man returned and was curious to know how the young man had fared in his first season as a fox-hunter. He was very surprised to find that the young hunter had not caught one single fox during the whole winter season. When the experienced fox-hunter asked the young man if he had followed the instructions he had been given, he replied, "No, I found a better way."

One reason we desired to come to earth is that, in our pre-mortal state, we saw how happy our celestial parents were, and we wanted to become like them. The gospel of Jesus Christ is the way to happiness and a fulness of joy. The world is filled with people who are not happy because they are seeking happiness by following what they feel is a "better way." Part of the problem is that many do not realize the difference between happiness and fleeting pleasure, so Satan easily guides them onto other paths. This problem was described well by Elder James E. Talmage:

The present is an age of pleasure-seeking, and men are losing their sanity in the mad rush for sensations that do but excite and disappoint. In this day of counterfeits, adulterations, and base imitations, the devil is busier than he has ever been in the course of human history, in the manufacture of pleasures, both old and new; and these he offers for sale in most attractive fashion, falsely labeled, *happiness*. In this soul-destroying craft he is without a peer; he has had centuries of experience and practice, and by his skill he controls the market. He has learned the tricks of the trade, and knows well how to catch the eye and arouse the desire of his customers. He puts up the stuff in bright-colored packages, tied with tinsel string and tassel; and crowds flock to his bargain counters, hustling and crushing one another in their frenzy to buy.

Follow one of the purchasers as he goes off gloatingly with his gaudy packet, and watch him as he opens it. What finds he inside the gilded wrapping? He has expected fragrant happiness, but uncovers only an inferior brand of pleasure, the stench of which is nauseating. . . .

Happiness [on the other hand] leaves no bad after-taste, it is followed by no depressing reaction; it calls for no repentance, brings no regret, entails no remorse; pleasure too often makes necessary repentance, contrition, and suffering; and, if indulged to the extreme, it brings degradation and destruction. . . .

Happiness is not akin with levity, nor is it one with light-minded mirth. It springs from the deeper fountains of the soul, and is not infrequently accompanied by tears. (*Improvement Era*, vol. 17, pp. 172–73; also cited in *Jesus the Christ* [Salt Lake City: Deseret Book Co., 1977], pp. 247–48.)

Since all of us desire happiness, we should ask ourselves the questions: Do I really believe that living the gospel of Jesus Christ brings happiness? If so, what can I do to live it better?

There are many reasons why we can have total trust that Heavenly Father's gospel plan will really bring us happiness. We have already discussed the first reason, which is that we are his children and he loves us. Because of this love, he will never ask us to do anything that will not eventually lead to peace and happiness for us or for those around us.

Another reason why we can have total confidence in the Lord and his plan has to do with his great knowledge and the source of the plan. Many seem to have the idea that God made up the commandments that he asks us to keep. Some feel that God made these commandments difficult so that they would be a test that would show who is worthy of a greater glory.

The truth is that God has come to understand which laws and actions bring happiness, and has tried to teach us what these are. The commandments are not things we have to do so God will want to bless us; they are eternal laws that will bless our lives as we live them willingly and completely. When we forgive others we are happier than when we hold a grudge — not just because God said so, but because it is true.

In the Doctrine and Covenants, we read that "truth is knowledge of things as they are, and as they were, and as they are to come" (D&C 93:24). In the Book of Mormon, we find Jacob's teaching: "The Spirit speaketh the truth. Wherefore, it speaketh of things as they really are, and of things as they really will be." (Jacob 4:13.) As we come to realize in our hearts that God really does love us, and as we come to better understand the greatness of his knowledge, our confidence that gospel living really will bring us happiness will grow and expand.

Because of God's great knowledge, his perspective is much broader than our own. Joseph Smith taught that the "past, present, and future . . . are continually before the Lord" (D&C 130:7). Jesus said that he knows all things, for all things are present before his eyes (see D&C 38:2). On the other hand, in this life each of us sees only the span of his mortal life.

Because of our limited perspective, when we view events that are happening around us it is easy to misunderstand them or make wrong assumptions. That is why it is so important to build our lives on the word of God. In Lehi's and Nephi's great vision of the tree of life, the tree represented the love of God, and those that partook of the fruit of the tree received "exceedingly great joy" (see 1 Nephi 8:10–12; 11:21–22). As these two prophets saw in this vision, the only way to overcome the temptations of the devil and enjoy the fruit of the tree was to "cling" to the iron rod, which represented the word of God (1 Nephi 8:24; 11:25).

The flood at the time of Noah is a good example of God's eternal perspective. Many see the Flood as an act of cruelty because they fail to view it with an eternal perspective as God does. If we look at the Flood carefully, however, we see that not all those involved were losers. It is true that the people generally had reached a point in their lives at which they would not respond to the gospel and apparently were beyond repentance; hence the Lord removed them to the spirit world where they could ultimately be taught the gospel with perhaps more chance of some of them accepting it. The young children of the wicked were winners—they were taken out of the world before they could become like their parents, and became heirs to the celestial kingdom. Similarly many righteous people who lived before the Flood were translated and joined the city of Enoch. Noah and his family got a fresh start in a sinless world, and their posterity came into an environment where they had a chance to learn and grow spiritually instead of into one that was totally evil.

As we ponder our own lives from a broader perspective, then, we can come to realize that our happiest moments have originated from service, unselfishness, and the bridling of our passions. It is especially easy to see the happiness that gospel living brings as we see others accept the gospel and change their lives. The Baders were just such a family.

Two missionaries had been enjoying a beautiful spring day until they knocked on the door of Mrs. Bader. She hadn't noticed the lovely day, and it soon became apparent that she didn't feel there was anything of beauty in the whole world.

As soon as the missionaries had introduced themselves, Mrs. Bader took over the conversation and proceeded to explain to them why life wasn't worth living. She told how her alcoholic husband had run away with another woman, but not before he had taught her eight- and nine-year-old sons some very bad habits. He had been out of work for some time and had taught the boys how to ransack the house to find the welfare check. He would then take the two boys down to the pub to drink with him instead of using the money for their food and other necessities.

After the father had left, the boys continued to develop the bad habits he had taught them, by stealing at school and from the local merchants. Eventually they were expelled from school. Their education seemed to be over before they had even become teenagers.

Mrs. Bader had become so discouraged and depressed that she had tried to kill herself on three separate occasions. On two of the attempts she had been declared dead on arrival at the local hospital. As she spoke to the missionaries, she cursed the doctors for bringing her back to life.

While one of the missionaries stood there, wondering how to get away, his companion said, "Mrs. Bader, we would like to come back tomorrow and tell you about the gospel and how it can bring you happiness."

The discussion the next day was not the kind you put on a missionary training film. As one of the missionaries was showing a filmstrip, a hand came out from under the couch and grabbed his leg. This was one of the sons introducing himself, and it was the only time the missionary had ever screamed in the middle of *Meet the Mormons*. The other son introduced himself by placing his fingers in front of the film-strip projector and forming shadow images of ducks, dogs, and other assorted animals on the screen. Things went down-hill from there, and the missionaries finally stopped the film-strip. Mrs. Bader apologized for her sons' behavior and the missionaries politely accepted. The missionaries did not give up, however, and another meeting was scheduled for the next day.

The next day a miracle happened—the boys were out somewhere. Mrs. Bader actually listened to a whole discus-sion, and even seemed receptive. But when she was chal-lenged to read the Book of Mormon, she had all sorts of reasons for not being able to. One was that, since her suicide attempts, she could not read for more than ten minutes with-out developing terrible headaches. One of the elders felt prompted to promise her that while she read the Book of Mor-mon she would not have any headaches.

When the missionaries returned the next day, she had read over half of the Book of Mormon. She told the missionaries that it was the first time in years that she had been able to read and not get sick. After praying about it, she received a spiri-tual confirmation that it was the word of God and, in spite of opposition from some of her family, she was baptized a week later.

As the missionaries laid their hands on Sister Bader's head to confirm her, they felt the same Spirit that had been direct-ing them throughout the conversion process. They blessed her that she would be healed of several physical problems that had been plaguing her for years, and from that time forward she was healed.

Teaching her two boys was quite a chore. After five or six weeks of constant tutoring, though, they were finally ready to be baptized and become members of the Church.

Sister Bader's story did not end there, however. Her husband returned home and was amazed at what had taken place in his family. His wife had changed from a depressed, negative woman with no personal pride or goals into an enthusiastic, happy woman who knew exactly what she wanted and who was trying to live each day to the fullest. Because of the change in his family, Mr. Bader soon listened to the missionaries and was baptized.

The gospel is more than just concepts and ideas. It is a true power in the lives of people that transforms them and fills their hearts with joy. It is the great plan of happiness, and God shares it with us because we are his children. Celestial life and happiness are synonyms in a very real sense, and the more celestial we become, the happier we are.

5

Consecrating
Our All

One of the greatest stumbling blocks to celestial growth can be the benefits the world seems to offer, such as physical possessions, fame, wealth, power, and luxury. Talking about those who will be cut off from the Lord's people in the last days, Jesus said, "They seek not the Lord to establish his righteousness, but every man walketh in his own way, and after the image of his own god, whose image is in the likeness of the world" (D&C 1:16). Part of this adoration of worldly things comes from a misunderstanding of who the real owner is.

President Kimball told the story of a friend of his who took him to his ranch. The man unlocked the door of a beautiful new car and said proudly, "How do you like my new car?" As they drove up to a new landscaped home, the friend said with great pride, "This is my new home."

They then drove up on top of a grassy hill, and the friend pointed out his vast domain to President Kimball. He said, "From the clump of trees, to the lake, to the bluff, and to the ranch buildings and all between—all this is mine. And the dark specks in the meadow—those cattle also are mine."

President Kimball then asked his friend from whom he had obtained it, and was told that the land had originally been gained through land grants from the government. President Kimball wondered how the government got it and what they paid for it.

A scripture came into the prophet's mind: "The earth is the Lord's, and the fulness thereof" (1 Corinthians 10:26). President Kimball then asked his friend, "What was the price? With what treasures did you buy this farm?" The answer was "money," and was followed with the question, "Where did you get the money?"

His friend answered that he had used his strength to earn the money. The prophet then asked him where he got his strength to toil. The friend mentioned food, which of course led to the question, "Where did the food originate?" The friend was still not willing to give God credit, and said his food came from the sun, the atmosphere, and from the soil and water. President Kimball then wanted to know who brought those elements here.

The prophet attempted to teach his friend a valuable lesson. He quoted him scriptures that show that "the riches of the earth" are the Lord's to give (D&C 38:39), and that the "earth is the Lord's" (Exodus 9:29). He quoted a passage from the book of Psalms: "Those that wait upon the Lord . . . shall inherit the earth" (Psalm 37:9).

President Kimball told his friend that the earth was more of a lease on which a rental was due than a title suggesting ownership, but his friend continued to claim that the land and physical possessions were really his.

Many years later, President Kimball saw his friend lying in his casket among the luxurious furnishings of his home. He saw his friend buried in a "tiny, oblong area the length of a tall man, the width of a heavy one."

Years later President Kimball saw the same estate, rich with grain, lucerne, and cotton, and the land seemed unmindful of the friend who had claimed it. (See *Ensign*, March 1981, pp. 4–5.)

Everything that we have really belongs to the Lord. Even the air that we breathe belongs to him, and our lives are preserved because he lends breath to us (see Mosiah 2:21). As we prosper, the Lord expects us to share with him and those around us. This is much easier to do when we realize that our possessions are not really ours anyway. This attitude of sharing is one of the most easily recognizable signs of a celestial person.

A few years ago, Elder L. Tom Perry paid tribute to his wife who had recently passed away. She was an excellent example of someone who understood the value of the things of eternity over the things of this world, and so she had no trouble giving her time or possessions to others. The Perry family had moved to California and, while they were preparing their finances so they could buy a home, they rented one which furnished the appliances they needed. They had to store their own appliances in their garage while they waited for the purchase of a home.

One evening, in sacrament meeting, the bishop appealed to the ward for assistance for those who had lost most of their belongings in a devastating flood. As Elder Perry drove into his driveway a few nights later, he saw a man tying their appliances onto his trailer. When he rushed into the house to find out what was happening, his wife said, "Oh, didn't I tell you? After sacrament meeting last week, I informed the bishop if anyone needed our appliances for flood relief, they could have them."

After many years of compassionate service and unselfish giving, Sister Perry contracted a terminal disease. As her life was filled with physical hardship, she seemed to become even more sensitive to the physical needs of others. She didn't want others to know about her illness, so only a few were aware of her personal suffering.

She had three serious operations in a short space of time, with only a few knowing she had been in the hospital at all. She would attend church on Sunday and have the operation early Monday morning. By Tuesday she would be trying to get out of bed, and by Wednesday would be moving around and trying to rebuild her strength. Thursday she would help the nurses assist others who were in the hospital, and she would spend Friday trying to convince the doctor to let her go home. Saturday the doctor would give in and discharge her, and Sunday morning she would be back in church looking radiant. Most of the people in the ward never knew she had been in the hospital having major surgery.

As Elder Perry would rush down after the meeting to take her home so she could get some needed rest, he would hear her say to someone else in need, "Now don't worry about a thing. I'll have dinner ready for you and at your home on Thursday night." (*Ensign*, May 1975, pp. 32–33.)

Sister Perry made the decision very early in her life to dedicate herself to the service of God and others, and her life was filled with satisfaction and joy because of it. We dedicate temples, chapels, and other church edifices to the building up of the kingdom of God. God has told us that our very bodies are temples, so why not consecrate and dedicate to him the most important temple of all—the temple of our spirit? Each of us is much more precious and valuable to God than any building, no matter how sacred the building may be. Long after other temples and chapels may have become rubble, the personal temples of our bodies will remain in a glorified, perfected state.

The words *consecrate* and *dedicate* mean to set apart for holy or special purposes. When we decide to dedicate ourselves to the Lord, we let him know that we will put his work first in our lives. We commit to put at his disposal our time, our talents, and everything that we own. Elder Boyd K. Packer described his own personal commitment to the Lord:

I . . . have come to know the power of truth and of righteousness and of good, and I want to be good. I'm not ashamed to say that—I want to be good. And I've found in my life that it has been critically important that this was established between me and the Lord so that I knew that He knew which way I had committed my agency. I went before Him and in essence said, "I'm not neutral, and You can do with me what You want. If You need my vote, it's there. I don't care what You do with me, and You don't have to take anything from me because I give it to You—everything, all I own, all I am." And that makes the difference. (*"That All May Be Edified"* [Salt Lake City: Bookcraft, 1982], p. 272.)

This attitude of dedicating all that we have and are to the Lord and his purposes is expressed many times every day by people of all ages. A young man from Asia was baptized while he was in the military, realizing that his family would disown him, that the army would give him no military rank, and that he would have a difficult time in school. An eighty-three-year-old man knelt by the bed of his dying wife and said, "Dear Father, if it be thy will, take my strength and give it to her; take my heartbeat and give it to her, that her heart might continue beating." A young man was offered a $28,000 Ferrari if he would stay home from his mission, but served a dedicated mission instead.

One young Elder and his family are representative of the numerous Church members who have dedicated their lives to the Lord. The Elder's family was so large that the father had to pick up a part-time job in order to support his son on his mission. They still did not have enough money, so the mother went to work in the school lunch program. The missionary still did not receive enough money, and fell a little further behind each month.

The mission president had a friend who occasionally gave him several $100 bills to share with missionaries who needed extra help. When the president interviewed the Elder, he found that the young missionary was really trying but was having a struggle financially. With a little prompting he found that this young man, in order to try to live on what he was receiving, had not eaten anything during the past three days. When the mission president handed him two crisp $100 bills and said that a friend had asked him to give them to him, the Elder was overcome.

Another example of commitment can be found in the case of Elder Sheffield, who, before his mission, had been operated on eleven times in major surgery and many more times in minor surgery. His one great desire as he grew up was that the surgery would make it possible for him to serve a mission. His final operation had been a year before he had entered the mission field and, in spite of severe pain and physical suffering, Elder Sheffield averaged between seventy and eighty hours a week in proselyting.

He was a great blessing and inspiration to the other missionaries, especially those who thought they had problems. One companion told the mission president that Elder Sheffield's shoulder fell out of place often and caused him severe pain. When the president suggested to Elder Sheffield that he check into a local hospital and have the problem corrected, he replied, "President, I have spent most of my life in hospitals, and when I complete my mission I am returning to several more major operations. I promised the Lord that if he would let me serve a mission, I would not spend one day in the hospital during the two years no matter how sick I was or how much I suffered." (See Vaughn J. Featherstone, *Ensign*, November 1978, p. 27.)

An important part of dedicating ourselves to the Lord is to be in tune with the Holy Ghost. Many times the Lord has different desires and goals for us than we may have for ourselves. One of my favorite stories illustrates the importance of making our decisions a matter of prayer, even though we feel we are doing the right thing.

When Heber J. Grant was an Apostle, he was asked by the President of the Church to collect funds to help save a major bank in Salt Lake from failing. Some people questioned the wisdom of the Church being involved, but Elder Grant went ahead as he had been directed.

When he visited Provo, he visited Jesse Knight and asked him for $5,000. He knew that Jesse Knight was a man of means and felt that he could do it. Jesse said, "No, I don't think that an Apostle of the Lord ought to be going out gathering funds for that purpose. I don't think that that's a worthy cause to go out and make collections for."

In spite of his conviction that saving the bank was not a worthy endeavor, Brother Knight was dedicated to the Lord and finally said, "I'll tell you what I will do. I will go home tonight, and I will pray to the Lord about that. And if I get the inspiration to give you that $5,000, I'll do it."

Brother Grant told him that he may as well give him the check now. "I am sure if you pray about it I'll get it," he said.

Two or three days later Brother Grant received a check from Brother Knight for $10,000. When they next met, Brother Grant asked Jesse what had happened, and received this answer: "I'll tell you this, Brother Grant. When you come to me again with a mission from the President of the Church to raise funds, I'm going to pay without any question. You're much more liberal than the Lord is. I went home as I promised to do, and I told the Lord that Heber was asking me for this contribution, and I wanted to know how he felt about it. I got down on my knees, and it just kept going through my mind like a tune: 'Give Heber $10,000.' And I got into bed and that tune kept going through my mind: 'Give Heber $10,000. Give Heber $10,000.' I got down on my knees again and said, 'Lord, Heber didn't ask me for $10,000. He only asked for $5,000.' The tune kept going through my mind. 'Give Heber $10,000. Give Heber $10,000.' And so, in order to satisfy the situation and have peace of mind, I told the Lord, 'Alright, I'll give him $10,000.'" (See Joseph Anderson, *Prophets of the Living God*, Brigham Young University Speeches of the Year [Provo, 29 July 1969], pp. 6–7.)

Turning our lives over to God is not really a sacrifice, but it is a great opportunity and blessing. President Ezra Taft Benson said: "Men and women who turn their lives over to God will find out that he can make a lot more out of their lives than they can. He will deepen their joys, expand their vision, quicken their minds, strengthen their muscles, lift their spirits, multiply their blessings, increase their opportunities, comfort their souls, raise up friends, and pour out peace. Whoever will lose his life to God will find he has eternal life." (*New Era,* May 1975, p. 20.)

The way to overcome the telestial world that we live in and develop the celestial qualities that we came here to acquire is to turn our lives over to God. Trying to ignore or avoid the enticements of the world can be discouraging and futile. Instead, as we fill our lives with the good things of life—the things that bring eternal life—we will find that the things of the world will lose the attraction they once had, and many of them will even become repulsive to us. A sense of order and purpose will fill our lives and bring us a peace and happiness that can come in no other way.

In President Benson's opening address of the April 1988 general conference he said: "When we put God first, all other things fall into their proper place or drop out of our lives. Our love of the Lord will govern the claims for our affection, the demands on our time, the interests we pursue, and the order of our priorities." (*Ensign,* May 1988, p. 4.)

6

Opposition—
Friend or Foe?

Misfortune and tragedy can come to anyone, regardless of his degree of faith or lack of it. Missionaries die while serving the Lord in the mission field. Parents die from cancer and other diseases, leaving small children motherless or fatherless. Young children are physically and emotionally abused by the very adults to whom they should be able to look for protection. Millions of people suffer and die from hunger, while others have plenty, and even excess. Almost every day, someone around us asks the question, Why?

Why didn't the Lord protect the young men that were serving him? Why does he allow parents to die and leave young children to be trained by others? Why does the Lord allow his children to suffer and die from starvation? Too many times these questions contain phrases of doubt, such as the following: If the Lord loves us, why does he allow so much misery and suffering to take place? If we are his children, why doesn't he respond to our desires and heal us? If there is a God, why does he allow children to suffer and die?

The suggestion is that God should show his love by protecting us from opposition of any kind.

If you examine these statements carefully, you may recognize that they are similar in their construction and tone to statements made by Satan and his followers approximately two thousand years ago. Satan questioned the divinity of Jesus when he said, "If thou be the Son of God, command that these stones be made bread" (Matthew 4:3). The soldiers at the Savior's crucifixion mocked him and said, "If thou be the king of the Jews, save thyself" (Luke 23:37). Even the thief on the cross said, "If thou be Christ, save thyself and us" (Luke 23:39).

As Jesus was beaten, spit upon, and humiliated in every way, many of his followers must have questioned why God would allow such things to happen. Both then and now, Satan wants us to perceive suffering and injustice as indications that God does not love us, or that there isn't a God at all. Yet there are reasons why God did not intervene at the time of Christ's suffering and crucifixion, and there are reasons why he intervenes only at certain times today.

The great prophet Nephi made a statement that shows the tremendous faith he had in our Father in Heaven. Nephi went through much tribulation in his own life, and was mocked and beaten many times by his brothers in spite of his own efforts and desires to live the gospel. When asked a question about God, Nephi answered, "I know that [God] loveth his children; nevertheless, I do not know the meaning of all things" (1 Nephi 11:17). We do not need to understand why God allows things to happen in order to know that God loves us. The very fact that he does allow suffering and sickness to occur should indicate that opposition is needed for celestial growth.

President Kimball wrote:

Being human, we would expel from our lives physical pain and mental anguish and assure ourselves of continual ease and comfort, but if we were to close the doors upon sorrow and distress, we might be excluding our greatest friends and benefactors. Suffering can make saints of people as they learn patience, long-suffering, and self-mastery. The sufferings of our Savior were part of his education. "Though he were a Son, yet learned he obedience by the things which he suffered; and being made perfect, he became the author of eternal salvation unto all them that obey him." (Hebrews 5:8–9.) (*Tragedy or Destiny?* [Salt Lake City: Deseret Book Co., 1977], p. 3.)

Indications show that, before we came here, we understood what trials we would face, and we accepted them. President Moyle observed: "We might well be assured that we had something to do with our 'allotment' in our pre-existent state. This would be an additional reason for us to accept our present condition and make the best of it. It is what we agreed to do. . . . We unquestionably knew before we elected to come to this earth the conditions under which we would here exist, and live, and work." (Henry D. Moyle, in Conference Report, October 1952, p. 71.)

President Kimball spoke even more explicitly about our pre-earth choices:

We knew before we were born that we were coming to the earth for bodies and experience and that we would have joys and sorrows, ease and pain, comforts and hardships, health and sickness, successes and disappointments, and we knew also that after a period of life we would die. We accepted all these eventualities with a glad heart, eager to accept both the favorable and unfavorable. We eagerly accepted the chance to come earthward even though it might be for only a day or a year. Perhaps we were not so much concerned whether we should die of disease, of accident, or of senility. We were willing to take life as it came and as we might organize and control it, and this without murmur, complaint, or unreasonable demands. (*Faith Precedes the Miracle* [Salt Lake City: Deseret Book Co., 1972], p. 106.)

The fact that God does not always heal the sick and protect the righteous does not mean that he leaves us alone. He blesses us with inspiration and revelation to help us solve the problems we face. He gives us the scriptures and counsel through inspired leaders to help us avoid misery and suffering. He fills our hearts with courage, strength, and peace through the ministering of the Holy Spirit. The following story illustrates well how blessings may come to us in the midst of tragedy.

Sharon, who was the oldest daughter of an active Latter-day Saint family, had recently returned from her mission to France and Belgium. She had decided to spend the summer in Anchorage, Alaska, with a former missionary companion. She worked at a Travelodge and had a wonderful summer.

In September her father received a phone call from Alaska informing him that Sharon and a friend had been on a plane that was missing. He was told that a storm had come up but that there was still a possibility that they were down safely somewhere.

Hoping he would soon find that they were okay, and wanting to spare his wife and younger children the anxiety that he was feeling, he decided to share his concerns with his oldest son only.

The next evening at about eleven o'clock, his daughter's girlfriend, Cindy, called to let him know that search parties had been out all day, but no wreckage or aircraft had been found. This meant that there was still hope that Sharon was safe. The search had ended due to darkness but would be resumed the next morning.

By this time the father felt he should inform his wife and the rest of the family, and they united together in fasting and prayer.

Considering this set of circumstances, we might ask ourselves these questions: Does God have the power to keep Sharon alive or bring her back to life? If we were Sharon's family, would God need to keep her alive in order for us to continue to have faith in him and believe that he really loves us? Is our love for and faith in God dependent on his blessing us, or will we trust and love him no matter what happens in our lives? In God's perspective, could anything good come to Sharon or someone else in the event of her death?

About nine o'clock the next evening, Sharon's family received a phone call from Cindy's father informing them that the plane wreckage had been found, and Sharon had been killed.

The entire family was stunned and grief-stricken, yet somewhat composed and comforted, except for a fourteen-year-old daughter named Mary Ellen. She simply could not accept the reality of Sharon's death, insisting that her sister was too young and too good to have been taken. The father tried to comfort Mary Ellen by expressing to her his faith in the plan of salvation. He reminded her that Sharon was one of those choice people who were well prepared for this step in their progression. With this assurance, Mary Ellen seemed quieter and went to her room.

Unknown to her family, Mary Ellen was still upset and wrote the following letter to the President of the Church:

Dear President Lee,

I don't want to take up your valuable time, but I need to ask a favor, if you please would.

This Thursday, my sister was found dead in an airplane out of Anchorage, Alaska. She had been missing since Tuesday. All our family had fasted and prayed for her. My father says that it is the Lord's will, and I would like to believe him, but she was so young and good. I've heard that sometimes people die when they still have work to do here.

What I would like to ask of you is, if you would pray, or have some other General Authority pray, to see if this is the right thing, or if she could be commanded to return. Whatever you tell me I would try to believe because you are a prophet of God.

Thank you for taking the time to read this.

Love,
Mary Ellen Hatch

Mary Ellen was calmer when she rejoined the family as they held hands and knelt down around the bed for family prayer that evening.

The family received phone calls throughout the next day from friends who wished to express their love and sympathy. About nine o'clock in the evening, the father answered the phone, and the voice on the other end said, "This is Harold B. Lee."

The father recovered from his surprise and summoned the other family members, who hurried to the four telephones they had at the house. With two at each phone they listened as President Lee expressed his love and his recognition of how they felt. He explained how he too had suddenly lost his own precious daughter, who had also lived in Provo. He went on to point out that the blessings that are promised to the faithful will not be curtailed because of the short span of mortality. He then assured them that all of Sharon's promised blessings would be received, and reminded them that birth into this life was not the beginning, nor death the end, of life in the eternities.

As President Lee hung up the phone, Mary Ellen ran into the kitchen and threw her arms around her father. She said, "Daddy, that's all I needed. He answered every question I had asked him in my letter!"

When her family asked her what letter she was referring to, she went into her room and returned with the letter. "I didn't mail the letter, Daddy," she said. "He must have heard the message from my heart!" (See Margie Calhoun Jensen, *Stories of Insight and Inspiration* [Salt Lake City: Bookcraft, 1976], pp. 118–21.)

God didn't protect Sharon from death, but he blessed her family in other wonderful ways. Most of us have not had the prophet call us in times of distress, but many of us can testify of times that the Spirit has blessed us with peace, understanding, and strength to go on, even though our prayers for deliverance for either ourselves or someone else have been declined. Carl and Launa are a good example of this.

As the nurses laid her newly born baby on the delivery

room table next to her, Launa watched his tiny lungs pull for all they were worth trying to get air. Being a nurse herself, Launa knew what it meant. She was fairly sure that her baby had Hiland Membrane disease, and she knew the death-rate at that time was ninety-eight percent. She felt that only with the help of God would her baby live.

Her husband, Carl, not realizing that the baby was sick, had hurried home to call all of the relatives and give them the good news. When he arrived back at the hospital he was shat-tered to find that his baby would probably not live through the night.

Carl called his relatives to ask them to fast and pray, and he spent the remainder of the night on his knees. He expressed to Heavenly Father how much he loved the child and prom-ised Him that, if He would allow his son to live, he would try to be a good father to him.

When Carl went back to the hospital, the doctors in-dicated that, if he was going to administer to his baby, he had better do it quickly. As Carl laid his hands on the baby's head, he was impressed to bless him to get well and to be able to come home. Four days later he came home with his mother.

The doctor was very surprised and said that he had never seen a baby recover from this disease like this baby had. Carl and Launa had chosen the name of David just in case they had a boy, but they changed the name to John, which means "a gift of God."

Several years later Launa was in the hospital again, this time with a seven-and-a-half-pound robust baby girl with fat cheeks, black hair, and beautiful eyes. Everything seemed fine with the baby except that she was fussy most of the time. Carl and Launa named her Lillian.

On the third morning (the morning Launa was to go home) the doctor examined Lillian and said that she had a heart murmur. She was sent immediately to the Primary Children's Hospital. Carl remembered how the Lord had blessed them when John was sick and began fasting and praying for Lillian. When he laid his hands on Lillian's head and asked permission from the Lord to bless her to get well like he had done for John, the Lord told him no. Lillian died during the night.

Carl was deeply troubled by this. On his way home from the hospital the next morning, he was crying. As he drove down the steep hill from the Primary Children's Hospital, he asked Heavenly Father that frequently asked question, Why? Why John and not Lillian? Why all the pain?

Then Heavenly Father did something very special for Carl. He showed Carl the reunion that he and Launa would have with Lillian. It was overwhelming, and Carl was immersed in the joy of that great hope. The feeling and vision and joy of being united again were so special that Carl had no more tears or sadness left.

During the first few days after Lillian's death, Carl was able to use the priesthood to bless Launa. He was able to speak at Lillian's funeral, dedicate her grave, and do many other things without stress or despair. Hopelessness did not engulf him. He and Launa were comforted and strengthened by the Lord.

One certainty of life is that each of us will be tested in some way. Just as building physical muscles demands resistance, spiritual growth needs opposition; just as Jesus suffered the pains of the flesh so that he would know "how to succor his people" (Alma 7:12), we too need these painful experiences to grow and develop and become like God. The important thing to realize is that we are never alone. President Ezra Taft Benson said:

God loves us. He's watching us, he wants us to succeed, and we'll know someday that he has not left one thing undone for the eternal welfare of each of us. If we only knew it, there are heavenly hosts pulling for us—friends in heaven that we can't remember now, who yearn for our victory.

This is our day to show what we can do—what life and sacrifice we can daily, hourly, instantly bring to God. If we give our all, we will get his all from the greatest of all. (*Ensign,* July 1975, p. 63.)

We do not need to understand the *why* of everything to know that God loves us and will help us. The next time we are asked why God allows suffering and heartache into the world, we can answer in words similar to Nephi's: I don't understand everything but there is one thing I do know, and that is that God loves us and does what is best for us.

7

The "Very Key"

In our quest for exaltation in the celestial kingdom, there are few things more important than how we use the God-given power to have children. If we use this power in the proper way in mortality and observe the Lord's other commandments, we will inherit this power for all eternity and will be gods. The Lord revealed that "in the celestial glory there are three heavens or degrees; and in order to obtain the highest, a man must enter into this order of the priesthood [meaning the new and everlasting covenant of marriage]; and if he does not, he cannot obtain it. He may enter into the other, but that is the end of his kingdom; *he cannot have an increase.*" (D&C 131:1–4, italics added.)

This power of procreation, then, is the core of our Heavenly Father's plan, both here in mortality and in eternity. Because of the importance of this eternal power, an understanding of the law of chastity is important for all people. It is not a topic that should be reserved for teenagers only. All of us need to evaluate our thoughts, desires, and behavior in this most important area.

Because of the importance of chastity and virtue, Satan works hard to promote immorality. The gap between what the world teaches and what God teaches is already a chasm, and it is growing wider each day.

Boyd K. Packer taught that how we use the sacred powers of creation is the "very key" to our happiness and to our becoming more like God. He explained:

There was provided in our bodies—and this is sacred—a power of creation, a light, so to speak, that has the power to kindle other lights. This gift was to be used only within the sacred bonds of marriage. Through the exercise of this power of creation, a mortal body may be conceived, a spirit enter into it, and a new soul born into this life.

This power is good. It can create and sustain family life, and it is in family life that we find the fountains of happiness. It is given to virtually every individual who is born into mortality. It is a sacred and significant power, and I repeat, . . . that this power is good. . . .

. . . It is a gift from God our Father. In the righteous exercise of it as in nothing else, we may come close to him. (*Ensign*, July 1972, pp. 111–12.)

On the other hand, the world teaches that this sacred power of procreation is only a physical appetite that should be satisfied along with all of our other appetites. Advertisements, jokes, literature, films, and everyday conversation all work together to degrade and cheapen this special power. Because Satan knows how important this sacred power is, he strives to make us misuse it.

Talking about Satan and his plan to cheapen this power, Elder Packer said:

In the beginning there was one among us who rebelled at the plan of our Heavenly Father. He vowed to destroy and to disrupt the plan.

He was prevented from having a mortal body and was cast out—limited forever from establishing a kingdom of his own. He became satanically jealous. He knows that this power of creation is not just an incident to the plan, but a key to it.

He knows that if he can entice you to use this power prematurely, to use it too soon, or to misuse it in any way, you may well lose your opportunities for eternal progression.

He is an actual being from the unseen world. He has great power. He will use it to persuade you to transgress those laws set up to protect the sacred powers of creation. (*Ensign*, July 1972, p. 112.)

It is interesting that one of the words the thesaurus gives as an opposite of the word *sacred* is *worldly*. The world would have us cheapen this sacred power. It can happen so subtly that, if we are not on guard, we may not even realize it is happening. We may find ourselves chuckling at off-color stories or watching TV shows and videos that would have appalled us several years ago. Slowly but surely, the teachings of the world can reach into our minds and hearts and cheapen how we feel about this sacred power.

The first step in staying morally clean is understanding just how important the law of chastity really is. The violation of this law has been described as second only to murder in seriousness; and although forgiveness is available to those who have transgressed this law, the repentance process required of such persons is not easy.

God's greatest concerns regarding mortality seem to be how we get into the world and how we get out of the world. The greatest sins include murder and immorality, and some of our greatest blessings come from respecting the sanctity of life and living the law of chastity. When a couple participates in the sacred act of procreation, they become partners with God in the creation of a human life. It is almost overwhelming when we realize that a spirit child of God is placed into a physical body that we create, and a living soul is born. Through this sacred physical union, divine individuals are introduced into their second estate.

Referring to this special link of co-creation that exists between us and God, Jeffrey R. Holland said the following:

Sexual intimacy is not only a symbolic union between a man and a woman—the uniting of their very souls—but it is also symbolic of a union between mortals and deity, between otherwise ordinary and fallible humans uniting for a rare and special moment with God himself and all the powers by which he gives life in this wide universe of ours. . . .

. . . I know of nothing so earth-shatteringly powerful and yet so universally and unstintingly given to us as the God-given power available in every one of us from our early teen years on to create a human body, that wonder of all wonders, a genetically and spiritually unique being never before seen in the history of the world and never to be duplicated again in all the ages of eternity: a child, *our* child—with eyes and ears and fingers and toes and a future of unspeakable grandeur. . . .

. . . I submit to you that no power, priesthood or otherwise, is given by God so universally to so many with virtually no control over its use except *self-control.* And I submit that we will never be more like God at any other time in this life than when we are expressing that particular power. (In Jeffrey R. and Patricia T. Holland, *On Earth as it is in Heaven* [Salt Lake City: Deseret Book Co., 1989], pp. 193–95.)

Once we realize the sacredness of sexual intimacy, we need to do those things that will ensure that it remains sacred to us. With the downward pull of the world, we need to plan ahead and have the help of the Lord in maintaining virtuous thoughts and actions. In a BYU devotional, President Benson gave six steps that he said would ensure that we would never fall in this area (see Ezra Taft Benson, "The Law of Chastity," *Brigham Young University 1987–88 Devotional and Fireside Speeches* [Provo, Utah: University Publications, 1988], pp. 49–54). The following steps, printed in italics, are President Benson's; the comments that follow are mine.

1. *Decide now to be chaste.* Think of the many benefits of being chaste both now and in the eternities. Make a firm decision to be chaste before you are in a situation in which it is difficult to think clearly. By making the decision now, you can completely avoid many threatening temptations.

2. *Control your thoughts.* A whole chapter of this book has been committed to this area because all of our actions, both good and bad, are but the outgrowth of our thoughts. Nothing destroys our good desires and intentions faster than not controlling our environment, and nothing helps us fulfill our desires more than being in places where the Spirit of the Lord can be.

3. *Always pray for the power to resist temptation.* Knowing of the great drawing power of the temptations of the world, God said, "Pray always, lest ye enter into temptation and lose your reward" (D&C 31:12). Especially important is to pray for the wisdom and strength to recognize and withstand the barrage of sexually demeaning material that is thrust upon us almost every day.

4. *If you are married, avoid flirtations of any kind.* In D&C 42:22, we read: "Thou shalt love thy wife [or husband] with all thy heart, and shalt cleave unto her [or him] and none else." The Lord has asked us to love only two people with all of our hearts: the Lord himself, and our spouses. Referring to this scripture, President Kimball explained:

When the Lord says *all* thy heart, it allows for no sharing nor dividing nor depriving. . . .

The words *none else* eliminate everyone and everything. The spouse then becomes preeminent in the life of the husband or wife, and neither social life nor occupational life nor political life nor any other interest nor person nor thing shall ever take precedence over the companion spouse. . . .

Marriage presupposes total allegiance and total fidelity. Each spouse takes the partner with the understanding that he or she gives totally to the spouse all the heart, strength, loyalty, honor, and affection, with all dignity. Any divergence is sin; any sharing of the heart is transgression. (*Faith Precedes the Miracle*, pp. 142-43.)

5. *If you are married, avoid being alone with members of the opposite sex whenever possible.* Situations that start out very innocently can sometimes quickly lead to tragedy when we find ourselves alone with a member of the opposite sex.

Some people say that this particular step is ridiculous. They feel that they have total control over their feelings and sexual drives under any circumstances. They are simply naive to the problems that arise daily among good people who place themselves in situations that they should and could have avoided.

One good man had served in bishoprics, had been on a high council, and had held many other important positions in the Church. He was sent on an assignment away from his home by his employer. A woman, who was also an active Church member, was also sent to this particular workshop by the same employer. After the meetings were over one evening, she asked him if he would like to come up to her hotel room for a few minutes and talk or play some games. Both were very innocent in their desires and were just bored with being away from home.

Their intentions were good but the setting and circumstances were wrong. One thing led to another until they both became unfaithful to their spouses and to God. Temple covenants were broken and heartache followed. Both returned home to tell their mates of their unfaithfulness, and innocent loved ones were injured. How much easier it would have been to follow the counsel of our leaders and avoid these situations altogether.

6. *For those who are single and dating members of the opposite sex, carefully plan positive and constructive activities so that you are not left to yourselves with nothing to do but share physical affection.* The combination of being alone and having nothing planned is simply a time bomb waiting to go off. None of us is strong enough to put him or herself in this kind of situation, night after night, with someone he or she is attracted to, without eventually having problems. High standards are important, as are wisdom and an understanding of our own physical drives.

One family had several daughters. As each daughter matured, she fell in love with a fine young priesthood holder and was sealed in a holy temple. Finally there was but one daughter left at home. This youngest daughter had looked up to her older sisters for as long as she could remember, and had set the goal for herself that she would follow in their footsteps and be married in the temple. She met a faithful returned missionary, and they fell in love. They had high standards and soon set a date to be married in the temple. The problem was that they were not very wise. They felt that, because of their standards and their love for one another, they could be alone and keep themselves clean and pure. With no planned activities of any kind, their nights together degenerated from pleasant conversation, to kissing, to necking and petting, and eventually to a complete loss of chastity and virtue. Their temple plans were scrapped, and the hearts of their parents and loved ones wounded. This couple married out of the temple and had to meet with their bishops to begin the painful but cleansing process of repentance.

Because of the immense importance of the power of procreation, and because of his great love for us, the Lord has revealed important safeguards to help shield and protect us in this critical area. It is vital for each of us to evaluate every activity in our lives to see if we are allowing the world's view of sex to infiltrate our thoughts or actions in any way. How we conduct ourselves in this area may have a greater effect, either positively or negatively, on our spiritual growth than what we do with respect to any other area of the gospel. Our proper use and protection of the power of procreation, both in thought and action, is one of the keys to our happiness here and in the world to come.

8

Turning Toward God

A few years ago several young men from Utah went to a Future Farmers of America (FFA) convention in Missouri. When they checked into their room, they found an advertisement for free food, bowling, and other games at a local bowling alley. They couldn't resist the word *free*, especially when it was connected with the word *food*, so they cleaned up and headed for the bowling alley.

As they ate and played games they were approached by members of a Christian church in the area. They found that this particular church had rented the bowling alley that evening and invited all of the FFA delegates to come and have a good time. The church had a worthwhile but misguided reason for the free food and games, which was, in their minds, to save the souls of all of the young men. They had printed cards with the words "I accept Jesus as my Savior. Therefore my sins are forgiven me and I am saved." At the bottom of each card was a place for a person to sign his name. When the young men questioned the validity of signing the card and having their sins forgiven, they were assured that this was all it would take. These young men are all adults now, but some of them still carry their cards in their wallets to indicate they have been forgiven.

Although repentance is one of the most basic and important Christian principles, it is also one of the most misunderstood. Although most Church members have a better understanding of repentance than those of other faiths, many have a misconception of what repentance really is. Elder Theodore M. Burton taught that it is sometimes easier to understand what repentance is not than to understand what it is:

Many times a bishop will write, "I feel he has suffered enough!" But suffering is not repentance. Suffering comes from *lack* of complete repentance. A stake president will write, "I feel he has been punished enough!" But punishment is not repentance. Punishment *follows* disobedience and *precedes* repentance. A husband will write, "My wife has confessed everything!" But confession is not repentance. Confession is an admission of guilt that occurs as repentance begins. A wife will write, "My husband is filled with remorse!" But remorse is not repentance. Remorse and sorrow continue because a person has *not* yet fully repented. Suffering, punishment, confession, remorse, and sorrow may sometimes accompany repentance, but they are not repentance. (*Ensign,* August 1988, p. 7.)

Repentance is a cooperative effort between us and the Lord. Most of us realize that gaining immortality and obtaining eternal life are major purposes of this life. Helping man gain these is the work and glory of God (Moses 1:39), but they need to become our work also if they are to be obtained. President Kimball observed: "Eternal life is a cooperative program to be developed by the Lord and his offspring on earth. It thus becomes the overall responsibility of man to cooperate fully with the Eternal God in accomplishing this objective." (*Miracle of Forgiveness*, p. 2.) We cannot repent and be forgiven of our sins until we decide to cooperate fully with God. Repentance is not just stopping something wrong or starting something right. The Greek word for repentance means "a turning of the heart and will to God and a renunciation of sin" (Bible Dictionary, LDS edition of the Bible, p. 760).

Repentance deals with our hearts and minds as well as our actions. Some may stop smoking or may attend church or help someone in need and still not turn their whole hearts and souls to God.

As Elder Burton explained, the Hebrew word for repentance means to "turn back to him [Heavenly Father]—to leave unhappiness, sorrow, regret, and despair behind and turn back to your Father's family, where you can find happiness, joy, and acceptance" (*Ensign*, August 1988, p. 7).

An interesting and thought-provoking scripture is one found in the book of James: "For whosoever shall keep the whole law, and yet offend in one point, he is guilty of all" (James 2:10). The first time many read this scripture they almost go into a panic, feeling they will have to live perfectly in order to be forgiven. Is this really what James means? Let us suggest another interpretation—that the key to understanding this scripture is to know what the law is that we need to keep in order not to be offenders.

During the last week of his mortal ministry, Jesus explained the law that requires our obedience: "Thou shalt love the Lord thy God with all thy heart, and with all thy soul, and with all thy mind. This is the first and great commandment. And the second is like unto it, Thou shalt love thy neighbor as thyself. On these two commandments hang all the law and the prophets." (Matthew 22:37–40.)

It seems, then, that the great law that we need to keep is to love God with all our hearts, souls, and minds, and our neighbors as ourselves. Every other commandment simply tells us how to love God and our fellowmen. If we love God, we will pay our tithing, treat others with compassion, and strive to do everything else God wants us to do. Jesus said, "If ye love me, keep my commandments. . . . He that hath my commandments, and keepeth them, he it is that loveth me." (John 14:15, 21.)

Repentance, then, is not something that can be done piece-meal. We are not forgiven of our sins one at a time. Repentance is a process of turning our attitudes, desires, and actions toward God, and when our hearts are pure and we are willing to do whatever God wants us to do, we are repentant and, therefore, forgiven. President Kimball taught:

Repentance must involve an all-out, total surrender to the program of the Lord. That transgressor is not fully repentant who neglects his tithing, misses his meetings, breaks the Sabbath, fails in his family prayers, does not sustain the authorities of the Church, breaks the Word of Wisdom, does not love the Lord nor his fellowmen. A reforming adulterer who drinks or curses is not repentant. The repenting burglar who has sex play is not ready for forgiveness. God cannot forgive unless the transgressor shows a true repentance which spreads to all areas of his life. (*Miracle of Forgiveness*, p. 203.)

This does not mean that the Lord expects us to live perfect lives, but he does expect us to want to and to try to. When we do everything we can do, placing the Lord first in our lives and continually repenting in order to improve, the atonement of Jesus takes effect in our lives.

In a very real sense, the process of repentance is the process of becoming celestial. It is a change within us that is then mirrored by our actions. According to the Book of Mormon record, after King Benjamin had taught his people, "they all cried with one voice, saying: Yea, we believe all the words which thou hast spoken unto us; and also, we know of their surety and truth, because of the Spirit of the Lord Omnipotent, which has wrought a mighty change in us, or in our hearts, that we have *no more disposition to do evil, but to do good continually*" (Mosiah 5:2, italics added). These people went on to say that they were willing to do God's will all the remainder of their days. They were not yet perfect, but they desired to be so and were willing to work for it; therefore, they were repentant and were forgiven of their sins. They had turned their hearts and efforts toward God, and were willing to cooperate fully with him in becoming celestial people. Section 76 of the Doctrine and Covenants teaches that celestial people are those who are valiant in their testimony of Jesus (see v. 51; compare v. 79), and explains that they are "just men *made perfect through Jesus the mediator*" (v. 69, italics added).

Our understanding of repentance is enhanced greatly when we understand two important laws: the law of justice and the law of mercy. The law of justice demands that for every law broken a penalty must be paid, and for every law kept a blessing is to be given. The law of mercy is a great gift that the Lord bestows upon us because of our weaknesses. The scriptures indicate that mercy cannot rob justice and that only the truly penitent can be saved. When we turn toward God with all of our hearts, the law of mercy comes into effect, which means that Christ's sacrifice atones for the sins that we have committed and thus delivers us from having to suffer ourselves. It is important to notice that someone has to fulfill the law of justice and pay the penalty, whether it be us or Christ. Because of the great love that Jesus has for us, he was willing to take our sins upon him. In a modern revelation, the Savior explained:

Behold, I, God, have suffered these things for all, that they might not suffer if they would repent;

But if they would not repent they must suffer even as I;

Which suffering caused myself, even God, the greatest of all, to tremble because of pain, and to bleed at every pore, and to suffer both body and spirit—and would that I might not drink the bitter cup, and shrink—

Nevertheless, glory be to the Father, and I partook and finished my preparations unto the children of men.

Wherefore, I command you again to repent, lest . . . you suffer these punishments of which I have spoken, of which in the smallest, yea, even in the least degree you have tasted at the time I withdrew my Spirit. (D&C 19:16–20.)

It is not surprising that we have to be trying to do our best in all areas of our lives in order to receive the full benefit of the Savior's atonement.

Elder Vaughn J. Featherstone related an experience that illustrates the importance of changing our hearts and attitudes, not just our behavior. He was asked to interview a young man who desired to serve a mission but who had been involved in a major transgression in his life. When Elder Featherstone asked him what the transgression was, the young man, with his head held high, said that there wasn't anything he hadn't done. When asked if he had been involved in fornication, he sarcastically answered that he had been involved with so many girls and so many times that he could not number them. He admitted proudly to using drugs and having committed other serious sins. Elder Featherstone's account continues:

Then I said, "What makes you think you're going on a mission?"

"Because I have repented," he replied. "I haven't done any of these things for a year. I know I'm going on a mission because my patriarchal blessing says I'm going on a mission. I've been ordained an elder, I've lived the way I should this past year, and I know that I'm going on a mission."

I looked at the young man sitting across the desk: twenty-one years old, laughing, sarcastic, haughty, with an attitude far removed from sincere repentance. And I said to him: "My dear young friend, I'm sorry to tell you this, but you are *not* going on a mission. Do you suppose we could send you out with your braggadocio attitude about this past life of yours, boasting of your escapades? Do you think we could send you out with the fine, clean young men who have never violated the moral code, who have kept their lives clean and pure and worthy so that they might go on missions?"

I repeated: "You're not going on a mission. In fact," I said, "you shouldn't have been ordained an elder and you really should have been tried for your membership in the Church."

"What you have committed is a series of monumental transgressions," I continued. "You haven't repented; you've just stopped doing something. Someday, after you have been to Gethsemane and back, you'll understand what true repentance is."

When Elder Featherstone met him again six months later, this young man was a different person. He had put his heart right and the Lord first in his life. He thanked Elder Featherstone for helping him get on the true road to repentance. (See *A Generation of Excellence: A Guide for Parents and Youth Leaders* [Salt Lake City: Bookcraft, 1975], pp. 156–59.)

The beginning of repentance for all of us is to commit ourselves completely to the Lord. Sometimes we seem afraid to commit our all, thinking we may have to give up something we really want, but in most cases God asks us to give up only those things that are stumbling blocks to our happiness. Just as the Savior put God's will ahead of his in the Garden of Gethsemane, we too can do the same, and eventually share with Christ and God all that they have.

9

Keeping Our Covenants

The story is told of the old farmer who traveled to town each week with farm produce which he traded to a merchant for things he needed. One day after the farmer left the store, the merchant happened to weigh a pound of butter the farmer had just left. He was surprised to find that it was one ounce short. He quickly weighed another pound and another, and found them all short by exactly one ounce.

When the farmer returned, the merchant told him of his discovery about the butter. He explained that a man who would stoop so low as to make his butter and cheese one ounce short of a pound just to get a little more out of it, wasn't the kind of person he cared to deal with.

The old farmer looked sad and said, "Well, we are just poor people. We don't own a pair of scales, so in order to measure how much cheese or butter to put into a pound we rigged up a sort of balance. We set a pound of sugar or rice that we have just bought from you on one side, and when the butter balances evenly, we figure it is a pound."

A teacher tells the story about a test he gave in high school. His brother was in his class, and when he corrected his paper he noticed that he had written "I don't know this one" in the space allocated for one of the answers. A few papers later, he corrected the test taken by his brother's friend, who happened to sit next to his brother. On the same question, he had written on his paper "I don't know this one either." (From *Love Letter* [periodical], July 1988.)

These stories approach the subject of dishonesty in a somewhat humorous way, but in actuality, dishonesty is very destructive, both to ourselves and to our relationships with others and God. There is nothing that erodes confidence and trust any quicker than dishonesty, and few things build respect and confidence better than honesty and integrity.

It is difficult to imagine a God that could not be trusted —a God that made promises and then didn't keep them. An indispensable quality in God's character is his unvarying honesty under all conditions and in all ages of time. In a revelation received by Joseph Smith, the Prophet was told that "God doth not walk in crooked paths, neither doth he turn to the right hand nor to the left, neither doth he vary from that which he hath said, therefore his paths are straight, and his course is one eternal round" (D&C 3:2).

Since the purpose of this life is to become like God, it is essential for us to become totally honest in all of our relationships. This includes our relationships in the Church, our families, and our work, and it means being truthful in our business transactions and in our dealings with the government. Most important, we must be totally honest in our relationship with God. For those who are actively working toward godhood, there is no such thing as selective honesty. There are those who will tell us that it is all right to deceive in our payment of taxes, or keep extra change, or make excuses for not keeping some promise that we have made. Some will tell us that we do not need to keep our word unless a contract was signed and officially notarized. Many seem to be able to justify themselves in cheating in sports, using supplies from work for personal use, and telling fibs or little white lies. Those who have made commitments to themselves and to God realize the importance of total honesty and integrity, no matter what the consequences. This is depicted well in the following story.

The very first Latter-day Saint that Mike ever met was Norman Taylor. He played on a soccer team with Mike and they called him "Norman the Mormon." His honesty and integrity made him unique among the young men on Mike's soccer team. Norman didn't smoke; he didn't drink beer, tea, or coffee; he didn't swear; and he didn't protest any referee's decisions.

One summer, Mike's team reached the English youth cup final for the first time in the team's twenty-five-year history. With less than five minutes to go in the championship game, the score was tied at a goal apiece. The other team was mounting attack after attack. Following a corner kick, the ball bounced off a couple of players and appeared to strike Norman on the hand. The other team immediately appealed for a penalty kick because of the hand-ball violation, while Mike's team denied their appeal.

Both the referee and linesman were unintentionally blocked by players from seeing the incident. The referee, knowing Norman's commitment to honesty and to his beliefs, asked him if he had touched the ball with his hand. Norman quietly answered, "Yes, I did." The referee awarded the other team a penalty kick, which was converted. Moments later the game was over, and Mike's team had lost 2–1.

As the team dejectedly filed into their changing room, not one player said an unkind word or made a scene as Norman sat with his face in his hands, quietly weeping at their loss. "Honesty," he said, "means more to me than anything. I'm sorry—sorry it cost us the game—but I was taught that honesty is a quality that remains with us for life. I can't turn it on and off just for a game."

Mike recollects that he and the team learned a great lesson that day, the lesson that honesty is one of the most valuable of all qualities and that it should always govern our actions, regardless of the cost. Mike later joined the Church and moved to Utah.

Norman is a young man who is well along the path of celestial growth. He has made commitments of honesty and integrity that seem able to withstand any pressure or expediency. He has also earned the respect of not only God but also players, officials, and spectators who have come in contact with him. Since the game, many parents and teachers have used his honesty and courage as an example. Although some people ridicule those who do what is right, most individuals respect and admire someone who can stand up for his convictions no matter what the consequences.

Many times, the pressures of the world are much greater than the desire to win a game. President N. Eldon Tanner told about a man who had to decide whether or not to keep his word when doing so would mean losing his house. He had made an agreement with a man that required him to make certain payments each year. He was in arrears and could not make those payments and pay for his house. He asked President Tanner what he should do, and President Tanner looked at him and said, "Keep your agreement."

"Even if it costs me my home?" the man asked.

President Tanner replied, "I'm not talking about your home. I am talking about your agreement; and I think your wife would rather have a husband who would keep his word, meet his obligations, keep his pledges or his covenants, and have to rent a home, than to have a home with a husband who will not keep his covenants and pledges." (See N. Eldon Tanner, in Conference Report, October 1966, p. 99.)

As we progress in our celestial growth, we find that our values improve. Behavior we would have considered permissible earlier in our lives begins to feel wrong. The Holy Ghost expands our vision and increases our sensitivity. We become less concerned about ourselves and the things of the world, and more concerned about God and others. Elder LeGrand Richards told of a convert who experienced this process:

A new convert in Florida also proved that he knew what the gospel is for . . . He was a fruit broker. He would purchase the entire crop of the various citrus groves and sell the same on the New York market. He said he thought he was a pretty shrewd broker, but after joining the Church, he began thinking of the shrewd deals he had made. So he left his home one day with his check book in his pocket, and called on his neighbors with whom he had done business. Upon his return to his home, he had spent $3,000.00. He said he then felt that he could look his neighbors in the face and tell them he was a Latter-day Saint. (*"Just to Illustrate"* [Salt Lake City: Bookcraft, 1961], p. 179.)

Even more important than being honest with others is being honest with God. Most of us have made many covenants or promises with the Lord. He will keep his word, and it is up to us to keep ours. The Lord said, "I, the Lord, am bound when ye do what I say; but when ye do not what I say, ye have no promise" (D&C 82:10).

Elder Boyd K. Packer wrote of an incident, told to him by an elderly member of the Church, that illustrates the importance of keeping covenants. As a youth this elderly brother had attended a funeral, and, Elder Packer relates,

the man who had died had not been active in the Church, although he was regarded as "a good man." He was a very close relative of the President of the Church. The members of the tiny farming community who gathered for the funeral were surprised and felt greatly honored that the President of the Church, the prophet, had come a long distance to the funeral. The first speakers commented on the virtues of the departed brother. One told of some acts of charity that he had done. He had given flour to widows, for instance. Other kindnesses were mentioned.

When it came time for the President of the Church to speak, his sermon was very unsettling to some. . . . The President first made an expression of appreciation for his deceased relative. He acknowledged the good that the man had accomplished and said he placed full value on those things that had been mentioned by the previous speakers. But then he said, "All of this may be well and good, but the fact is he did not keep his covenants."

The President then soberly outlined the fact that this man had been to the temple, that he had made covenants. But he had not kept them. He had fallen into inactivity in the Church and had developed habits and attitudes not in keeping with the priesthood he held. Those things he had done this side of the veil that were not in harmony with his covenants, and those things that he had not done this side of the veil that were required by his covenants, stood in the way of his eternal progression. These matters would need to be settled before he could claim the blessings of his covenants. He had not kept his part of the promise. (*The Holy Temple* [Salt Lake City: Bookcraft, 1980], p. 160.)

When we keep our covenants, blessings come to us now as well as later. The Lord said, "But learn that he who doeth the works of righteousness shall receive his reward, even peace in this world, and eternal life in the world to come" (D&C 59:23). There is no greater reward than being at peace in a world of turmoil. President Kimball observed:

Such peace comes only through integrity. When we make a covenant or agreement with God, we must keep it at whatever cost. . . . Let us not be like the missionary who agrees to serve the Lord for two years, then wastes his time with laziness and rationalization. Let us not be like the Church member who partakes of the sacrament in the morning, then defiles the Sabbath that afternoon by cleaning the house or by watching television or by choosing an afternoon of sleep over an afternoon of service. Instead, let us have integrity like Abraham did, observing with all soberness the solemn contracts we have made with God. (*Ensign*, June 1975, p. 6.)

President Kimball also taught that the most important word in the dictionary could well be *remember*. He said that we have all made covenants, and now our greatest need is to remember: "That is why everyone goes to sacrament meeting every Sabbath day—to take the sacrament and listen to the priests pray that they may 'always remember him and keep his commandments which he has given them.' . . . 'Remember' is the word. 'Remember' is the program." (*Circles of Exaltation* [address delivered to department of seminaries and institutes of religion, Brigham Young University, 28 June 1968], p. 8.)

Sometimes sacred and profound concepts can be taught to us by small children. Elder Harold B. Lee once related a story told to him by a temple watchman, a story about some children who had a keen sense of the sacred. The watchman's account reads as follows:

One morning not so long ago I was sitting at the desk in the temple gate house reading when my attention was drawn to a knock on the door. There stood two little boys, ages about seven or eight years. As I opened the door, I noticed that they were poorly dressed and had been neither washed nor combed. They appeared as if they had left home before Father or Mother had awakened that morning. As I looked beyond these little fellows, I saw two infants in pushcarts. In answer to my question as to what they wanted, one of the boys pointed to his little brother in the cart and replied: "His name is Joe. Will you shake hands with little Joe? It is little Joe's birthday—he is two years old today, and I want him to touch the temple so when he gets to be an old man he will remember he touched the temple when he was two years old."

Pointing to the other little boy in the other cart, he said this: "This is Mark, he's two years old, too." Then, with a solemn, reverent attitude rare in children so young, he asked: "Now can we go over there and touch the temple?" I replied: "Sure you can." They pushed their little carts over to the temple and lifted the infants up, and placed their hands against that holy building. Then as I stood there with a lump in my throat, I heard the little boy say to his infant brother, "Now Joe, you will always remember when you was two years old you touched the temple." They thanked me and departed for home. (As cited by Harold B. Lee, in Conference Report, April 1957, p. 21.)

The greatest reason of all for remembering and being true to our promises to God and others is so we can be true to ourselves. When we live true to the light and truth we have been given, we feel within us a sense of peace and unity, and we enjoy feelings of self-worth and self-respect. When we are dishonest, we find ourselves apprehensive and fearful, and our self-esteem plummets.

Paul taught that "he that committeth fornication sinneth against his own body" (1 Corinthians 6:18). Any sin we commit, including dishonesty, or lack of integrity, is a sin against ourselves. It may hurt others, but it damages us the most. In the book of Alma we read that all those who are cursed bring it upon themselves (Alma 3:6–19).

A few years ago, some money was stolen from an LDS seminary classroom. It was apparent that one of the seminary students had stolen it, since no one else had been in the room during the day. The next day the teacher prepared a lesson on the worth of a soul. He asked the students how much their souls and self-respect were worth to them. Were they worth more than a dollar? Were they worth five dollars or ten dollars or a thousand dollars? The teacher then indicated that someone had sold his or her soul the day before for less than five dollars. He said that if the perpetrator would like to clear his conscience and feel good about himself again, he could return the money and confess his sin.

Fifteen or twenty minutes after school let out, a young man walked hesitantly into the teacher's office. He confessed that he had stolen the money and had not felt good about himself since. He wanted to clear his conscience and be able to look the teacher in the eyes again without feeling guilty and anxious. The teacher and the student hugged and the student went away with a feeling of peace and of expanded self-worth.

Our quest for celestial life is one of not just doing, but of becoming. One of the most important qualities we need to develop is honesty—honesty with others, with God, and with ourselves.

10

The Celestial Triangle

Once we know—really know—that we are sons and daughters of God, this knowledge can forever change the way we feel about ourselves and others. It can bring to us feelings of self-respect and individual worth, and give us a self-confidence that can come from no other source. Knowing we are all children of God also brings the realization that we are truly brothers and sisters. This realization causes us to love others more and instills in us the desire to help those around us be more successful and happy. We would never willingly hurt a brother or sister whom we love.

These relationships are based on what the scriptures refer to as faith, hope, and charity—three qualities that are very interrelated, as illustrated by this description by Arthur R. Bassett:

My understanding of the atonement moved from my intellectual understanding to my emotional realm, and changes began to occur. I *wanted* to become what I sensed Christ knew I could be. Hope began to filter into my life, and my self-confidence increased. As my faith in Christ increased, my hope for my own situation also increased.

My capacity for charity increased with my increase in hope. Having received love myself, I found it easier to give in return. As I came to suspect that I had something to offer, I came also to realize not only an *obligation* to serve, but a *desire* to serve. I felt, consequently, a new sense of worth. With each new success, my faith in the Master and his way of doing things increased.

Somehow these three principles—faith, hope, and charity—seemed closely integrated and interrelated, each drawing strength and reinforcement from the others. . . . I felt good about God (faith), I felt good about myself (hope), and I felt good about others (charity). (*Ensign*, April 1979, p. 9, italics in original.)

A seminary teacher was once given an unusual class to teach. Over sixty ninth-grade students needed to be divided into two classes, and since neither teacher knew any of the students, they were divided randomly. The teacher who did the dividing felt that it might matter which group of students each teacher received, so he prayed and asked the Lord to direct which class he should teach. Following the prayer, he felt prompted to take the students in what we will call group A.

The next day, when the students arrived, to the amazement of both teachers, the classes were completely different. Group A consisted of students who physically as well as spiritually radiated little gospel knowledge or training. The other class was almost totally made up of vibrant, active Latter-day Saints who were eager to learn the gospel.

It only took three or four days for the teacher of group A to realize that he was facing the challenge of his career. He had already found that over half of his class of fourteen- and fifteen-year-olds had no idea who Joseph Smith was. While watching their first video, which referred to moral cleanliness, several of the girls raised their hands and asked if immorality was a very serious sin. He soon learned that the majority of his students came from broken homes, and that many of them were living in poverty. Some of his students were being physically abused at home, and most of them had received little or no training in the gospel. He overheard several of the girls talking about temple marriage and was shocked to hear them indicate that not one of them wanted to be married in the temple.

These and other experiences caused this teacher to get on his knees in prayer and ask the Lord what he should do to help these students. The answer came very clearly to his mind and heart. His primary objective for the year should be to help them realize that they were children of God, individuals of great potential and worth. He was to teach them that God loved them no matter what they had done or how others had treated them. He realized that if he could love them, and they could feel his love, they would then know that Heavenly Father could also love them since the Lord was more kind and loving than he was.

Every lesson was taught with the purpose of showing God's love for them. Over and over again he used the scriptures and modern-day examples to show the students that they really were children of God. Every day he tried to express his love for them verbally as well as by his actions. He taught them that because he loved them, he would discipline them and help them to learn self-control. He expected them to perform, and he rewarded them when they did. He taught them the importance of courtesy and of showing love for each other.

A turning point in the class took place the day that an especially "hard to love" boy raised his hand. This was a boy that most of the students and all of the teachers at the junior high school disliked very much. He said, with every member of the class listening, "Why do you love me? I have never had a teacher before that even liked me. Even my first grade teacher hated me. You are the only teacher I have this year that likes me. Why do you love me?"

The teacher was so grateful that this young man had felt his love, and silently asked the Lord to help him express why he loved him. The Spirit directed his words and he said,

"Bobby, I love you because you are my eternal brother. We lived together in the premortal existence, and I know we are related. I love you because I have prayed that Heavenly Father would fill my heart with love for you and for all of the other students in the class. Heavenly Father has answered my prayer and helped me to know that you are a royal person of noble birth with a great future before you if you will respond to him. Bobby, I love you for what you are now and for what I know you can become."

As the teacher finished telling Bobby why he loved him, a quiet, peaceful reverence permeated the classroom, and each person there knew that he or she was loved also. If the teacher could love Bobby, he could love anyone. By the end of the year these students knew that they were loved by their Heavenly Father, and with this knowledge came a quiet confidence that they were individuals of royal birth and of great worth.

These feelings of self-worth and confidence are what the scriptures call hope. Hope is the opposite of despair and discouragement. As these students increased their faith in God, and as their understanding of him and of their relationship to him grew, their feelings of self-worth and confidence (hope) increased. Although there seem to be many temporary sources of self-confidence, its permanent roots are found in obedience to the gospel. In the Doctrine and Covenants, the Lord said, "Let thy bowels [innermost feelings] also be full of charity towards all men, and to the household of faith, and let virtue garnish thy thoughts unceasingly; then shall thy *confidence* wax strong in the presence of God" (D&C 121:45, italics added). If we can feel confident in the presence of God, we can feel confident in the presence of anyone. Stephen R. Covey wrote:

Jesus taught that those who keep the Father's commandments will receive the Father's love, and will abide in his love. (See Jacob 3:1–2; Mosiah 4:12; John 14:21; John 15:10.) I believe this to be the perfect source of a divine definition of oneself. The main source of distorting this eternal sense is personal transgression, for even though the Father continues to love us unconditionally, we may not feel that love. He may give the gift but we do not receive it. . . .

. . . To live a life that is congruent and harmonious with Jesus Christ, our Savior and Redeemer, is the highest source of intrinsic security. (*Spiritual Roots of Human Relations* [Salt Lake City: Deseret Book Co., 1978], pp. 84, 89.)

The following story illustrates well how faith and righteous living can lead to feelings of hope, security, and self-worth.

Carl was a boy whose very existence was a struggle. He had a difficult time learning and was held back twice in school before he reached the third grade. He especially had a hard time learning to read and would cry himself to sleep, pleading with the Lord to help him to read and to learn.

When Carl's fourth grade teacher told him that she was going to hold him back another year, he pleaded and begged her to let him pass. He was already called stupid by many of the other kids his age and was especially ridiculed at home. His mother constantly told him he was stupid and worthless, and the rest of the family seemed to agree. He still remembers the day that his brother introduced him to his friend: "This is my stupid brother—he was held back twice."

When Carl's fourth grade teacher saw the emotional turmoil Carl was feeling, she told him that she would help him but that, among other things, he had to be able to pass his multiplication tables in order to move on to the fifth grade. Every day at lunch and after school she sat down with him and helped him until the day arrived for the final test. The test was timed, and while Carl was taking it, he realized that he would never be able to answer all the questions, so he put his head down on his desk and just cried. His teacher looked through the window and signaled him to finish. The next day she told him that he had passed and would be moving into the fifth grade. This teacher was the first person to really love Carl and try to help him.

Carl's life did not improve much between the fourth and seventh grades. He was failing his classes and his feelings of personal worth were almost non-existent. Then a miracle took place in his life. During his eighth grade year he moved in with his grandmother who lived in a small town. She was a quiet lady who radiated a sweet, loving spirit.

One day she gave him a book to read named *Principles of the Gospel*. Although it was a short book, it took him three months to read it. He would come home from school and go upstairs to a quiet room where he could be alone. This time in his life became one of study, pondering, and fasting and prayer. He was away from the yelling and name-calling and negative input that he had grown up with.

At the same time something unusual happened at school. The school had too many students and asked the Church to offer a special eighth grade seminary class, which they did.

As Carl learned about the gospel in seminary and read *Principles of the Gospel*, things started to change. He received a testimony and started to feel better about himself and what he could accomplish. His feelings of discouragement began to be replaced by feelings of hope. During those months in his grandmother's home, the Lord helped him gain stability, spirituality, and direction in his life.

One day after school Carl opened his sock drawer and found a Joseph Smith pamphlet. He didn't know where it came from, but he felt warm and calm as he held it in his hand. Somehow he knew that something important was about to happen, and he sat on the edge of his bed and started to cry.

He opened the pamphlet and, slow as he was, he didn't stop until he had read it from cover to cover. He then knelt down by his bed and prayed about the Prophet Joseph. He received a marvelous outpouring of the Spirit that has strengthened him throughout the rest of his life.

By the time Carl finished high school, he and the Lord had turned his life around. He earned straight A's his senior year, and received the great honor of being selected as a Sterling

Scholar. As soon as he graduated, he left for the mission field, where he served a successful mission. Since that time, Carl has received both a bachelor's and a master's degree and is a very successful teacher in the seminary program. Carl is an avid reader today and has paid the price to become a real gospel scholar. He is also one of the kindest and most loving individuals anyone could meet.

It is easy to see Carl's progression from faith to hope and then to charity. As he came to feel good about God and his relationship with him (faith), he started to feel better about himself (hope), which led him to serve others (charity). The main reason Carl wanted to be a teacher was because of the love he had received from his fourth grade teacher and from his seminary teacher. He wanted to be able to help young people who were struggling with some of the same kind of problems he had.

Faith, hope, and charity, however, do not always develop in that order. They interrelate with one another. Many times, charity leads to an increase in hope and faith.

This was the experience of Jeanette Schies, who was a member of the Church, but had become less active and rebellious, and was filled with bitterness and despair.

When Jeanette was nineteen years old, her mother passed away. Her father married a woman of another faith and, along with Jeanette's four brothers and one sister, joined his new wife's church. Jeanette became very lonely and was eventually filled with unhappiness and despair. She married a less active member which led to further inactivity and eventually to feelings of rejection.

Her life began to change the day her bishop asked her to teach a Primary class. She could tell by the look on his face that he wasn't going to leave until she accepted, so she agreed, thinking that she would teach for a week or two and then quit. She found out, however, that she liked the kids and, as she continued to teach, she grew to love them. One of the things that helped her the most was that they accepted her without reservation.

A few months later, the Relief Society president asked her to be a visiting teacher, but Jeanette didn't feel ready to make such a commitment to the Church. When the president asked her to reconsider, Jeanette half-jokingly said, "Maybe, but only if you give me someone who is totally incapacitated who would be a captive audience and who couldn't kick me out."

To her surprise, she was assigned three women who fit that description: an elderly woman who was bedfast and two women who were in a rest home.

She decided to visit them once a week and brought them flowers each time she came. As she laughed and cried with her three older friends, the pains of loneliness that she had carried from the loss of her mother began to diminish.

During her weekly visits to one of her friends in the rest home, she could not help but notice the old woman who shared the same room. The woman's face was covered with warts and moles, and her hair was dirty and straggly. She would always snap at Jeanette while she was trying to visit her friend. Jeanette noticed that this old woman never had any visitors of her own. Because of her grouchy disposition, the nurses sarcastically called her "Mrs. Sunshine."

Jeanette started bringing a flower to "Mrs. Sunshine" each time she came, and it wasn't long until she noticed a thawing process taking place. Then one morning, as Jeanette entered the room, she found "Mrs. Sunshine" asleep. She reached over and held her hand, and the Spirit told her to kiss her cheek. As she bent down and kissed her, "Mrs. Sunshine" threw her arms around Jeanette's neck and started to cry. She said, "No one ever kissed me before. I'm so ugly."

Jeanette sincerely told her that she felt she was beautiful. Jeanette recalls what happened next: "Suddenly all the bitterness and resentment and loneliness I had been harboring for years melted away. I felt pure love pouring into me, healing my heart. For the first time, I saw 'Mrs. Sunshine' and myself through the eyes of the Savior."

Reflecting on her relationship with "Mrs. Sunshine," Jeanette observes, "She had helped me grow closer to the

Spirit, and I had developed a greater capacity for love. No longer could I meet someone without seeing some of his or her worth and potential. As a result, I had begun to understand and appreciate my own worth in the eyes of God, and my confidence had grown stronger.

"With my newfound self-esteem, I desired to reach out to others. I received a firmer testimony of the gospel's power to change hearts and minds." (See *Ensign*, August 1988, pp. 47–49.)

Notice that through service and love, Jeanette received hope and faith which led to an even greater desire to serve others. As we reach out and serve others, our own faith, love, and hope will increase, and we will become more and more like our celestial parents and our brother Jesus Christ.

11

Pondering—Inner
Conversations with God

Many of the great experiences and revelations recorded in the scriptures were associated with pondering and meditation. Nephi was pondering his father's vision of the tree of life when he was "caught away" in the Spirit. He saw many great things, including Mary, the mother of Jesus, and the baptism, ministry, and crucifixion of Christ. (See 1 Nephi 11.)

Joseph Smith and Sidney Rigdon were working on the new translation of the Bible when they came across a scripture that discussed the resurrection of the just and the unjust. The Holy Ghost caused them to marvel and, as they meditated upon what they had read, they saw Jesus and angels and received the vision of the three degrees of glory. (See D&C 76.)

After Jesus' baptism he spent forty days preparing himself for his ministry by communing with God in the wilderness. This time of great meditation prepared him for the temptations of Satan that immediately followed. (See Matthew 4.)

When Jesus visited the Book of Mormon people following his resurrection, he taught them many great things and then commanded them to go to their homes and ponder upon the things he had said (see 3 Nephi 17:2-3).

Other great revelations such as the Word of Wisdom (D&C 89) and the vision of the redemption of the dead (D&C 138) were direct results of pondering. The fact that pondering and meditation played such an important part in the lives of the prophets and the Savior is not surprising when we consider President David O. McKay's teachings about the importance of meditation:

I think we pay too little attention to the value of meditation, a principle of devotion. In our worship there are two elements: One is spiritual communion arising from our own meditation; the other, instruction from others, particularly from those who have authority to guide and instruct us. Of the two, the more profitable introspectively is the meditation. Meditation is the language of the soul. It is defined as "a form of private devotion, or spiritual exercise, consisting in deep, continued reflection on some religious theme." Meditation is a form of prayer. . . .

Meditation is one of the most secret, most sacred doors through which we pass into the presence of the Lord. (In Conference Report, April 1946, p. 113.)

When we receive instructions from others, it is usually received as we meet in groups, and is given in broad terms of principles and standards. Even the scriptures have been designed to speak to a wide spectrum of people with different needs and desires. As we learn to ponder and meditate, however, the Holy Ghost speaks to our minds and hearts and personalizes what we have been taught or have been studying. The Holy Ghost, in a sense, becomes our personal tutor, and we receive individualized instructions from the Lord.

Our celestial growth becomes much more effective when we add pondering to our scripture study and prayer. Sometimes we get so caught up in the pressures and commitments of the world that we almost compartmentalize God and our communication with him. We make a five-minute appointment with him for prayer and possibly set aside another fifteen minutes for scripture study, unless something else interferes. Even worse, as soon as our appointment with God is over, we may move on to other pressing business without giving a second thought to what we read from the scriptures or discussed in our prayer.

A woman named Barbara was a successful businesswoman who was happily married and had three teenagers. Even though her life seemed to be going well, she felt an emptiness but did not understand why. One day she shared her feelings with a friend, who spoke to her of the "need to fit [one's] life around God." Her friend concluded, "The idea is to take a chunk of time big enough to mean something to you — and then, give that chunk to God."

Barbara decided to apply her friend's advice and got up early one morning to pray. Since she had an hour she found that her thoughts wandered, but eventually she relaxed and became more aware of the quiet sounds that surrounded her. She describes what happened next: "Then I felt the warm presence of love. I know no other way to describe it. The air, the very place in which I sat, seemed to change, as the ambiance of a house will change when someone you love is home.

"I had been sitting for 50 minutes, but only then did I really begin to pray. And I discovered I wasn't praying with my usual hurried words or my list of 'gimmies.'"

After having spent an hour a day in pondering and prayer for six years, Barbara concludes, "Starting my day with an hour of prayer has filled the empty space — to overflowing." (Barbara Bartocci, "One Hour That Can Change Your Life," *Reader's Digest*, March 1984, pp. 13–16.)

As Barbara added meditation to her prayers, her happiness and peace increased. Meditation and prayer, however, do not need to be limited to a certain time of the day nor should they be isolated from our other responsibilities and activities. Barbara's friend advised her to fit her time around

God instead of expecting God to fit his time around her. Even better would be to share her time with God so they could be together throughout the day. Amulek taught the Zoramites that we should and could pray continually:

Yea, cry unto him for mercy; for he is mighty to save.

Yea, humble yourselves, and continue in prayer unto him.

Cry unto him when ye are in your fields, yea, over all your flocks.

Cry unto him in your houses, yea, over all your household, both morning, mid-day, and evening. . . .

Yea, cry unto him against the devil, who is an enemy to all righteousness.

Cry unto him over the crops of your fields, that ye may prosper in them.

Cry over the flocks of your fields that they may increase.

But this is not all; ye must pour out your souls in your closets, and your secret places, and in your wilderness.

Yea, and when you do not cry unto the Lord, let *your hearts be full, drawn out in prayer unto him continually for your welfare,* and also for the welfare of those who are around you. (Alma 34:17-21, 23-27, italics added.)

James T. Duke, a professor at Brigham Young University, suggests that thinking is simply a conversation that we have with ourselves. We say things to ourselves such as: "It's time for me to put out the garbage." "I wonder how Dave is doing?" "I hope I have enough gas to get to work."

Brother Duke proposes that by including God in our thoughts—in our conversations with ourselves—we can apply the teachings of Amulek and pray continually. He gives the following example of including God in our thoughts:

"I wonder how Dave [a missionary son] is doing today. Father, please watch over David today and keep him safe. Please lead him to those who are seeking thy gospel. And thanks for letting me raise that fine son, and for his goodness and willingness to serve thee. Wow, I'd better get going or I'll be late for work." (*Ensign*, February 1987, p. 25.)

What Brother Duke describes is a form of pondering, and it brings us much closer both to God and to those whom we ponder about. As mentioned earlier, scripture study is also an integral part of the pondering process. As we ponder the truths and situations in the scriptures, the Holy Ghost helps us obtain new insights, enrich our lives, and increase our spiritual growth.

Pondering and meditation can also lead us to new truths, help us find solutions to daily problems, and bring greater peace and understanding to our souls. Joseph Smith described the pondering process well:

"In the midst of this war of words and tumult of opinions, I often *said to myself:* What is to be done? Who of all these parties are right; or, are they all wrong together? If any one of them be right, which is it, and how shall I know it?" (Joseph Smith—History 1:10, italics added.)

Joseph's thoughts and desires were focused on finding the truth. In his search for truth he turned to the scriptures.

"I was one day reading the Epistle of James, first chapter and fifth verse, which reads: *If any of you lack wisdom, let him ask of God, that giveth to all men liberally, and up-braideth not; and it shall be given him*" (Joseph Smith—History 1:11, italics in original).

Joseph did not read the scriptures and then forget about them as he went about his daily responsibilities; spiritual matters were not put on hold until the next appointed time for study. His account reads:

Never did any passage of scripture come with more power to the heart of man than this did at this time to mine. It seemed to enter with great force into *every feeling* of my heart. I *reflected on it again and again,* knowing that if any person needed wisdom from God, I did. . . .

At length I *came to the conclusion* that I must either remain in darkness and confusion, or else I must do as James directs, that is, ask of God. I at length came to the *determination* to "ask of God." (Joseph Smith—History 1:12–13, italics added.)

Pondering led to scripture study and prayer which, along with more pondering, led to discovering the truth. Recently a young mother made the decision to get more out of her temple visits. As a general rule, when she had sat through the endowment sessions in the past, her mind had wandered, and many times she had felt sleepy. Others had told her that they learned something new almost every time they went, so one day she decided to listen intently, pray for the Spirit, and see if she could gain some new insights or understanding.

When she left the temple that day, she had no new answers, but her mind was filled with new questions. At first she felt somewhat disappointed, but as she pondered the questions that had come to her in the temple, the Spirit helped her understand concepts that were new and spiritually exciting to her. Through her pondering, she found greater truth and understanding.

Section 9 of the Doctrine and Covenants suggests that prayer without pondering is not enough. The Lord told Oliver Cowdery: "Behold, you have not understood; you have supposed that I would give it unto you, when you *took no thought* save it was to ask me. But, behold, I say unto you, that you must *study it out in your mind;* then you must ask me if it be right." (D&C 9:7–8, italics added.)

God does not seem to be suggesting that we sit around and do nothing but meditate; rather, he seems to be saying that we need to plan our lives so that we have opportunities to consider the things of real importance. Referring to his words, Jesus said, "Treasure these things up in your hearts, and let the solemnities of eternity rest upon your minds" (D&C 43:34). There are many times during the day when we can meditate if we desire to do so. If the TV and radio are turned off while housework is being done, the mind is free to think of other things. Time spent waiting and driving, which for many of us is considerable, can be made more productive. All of us can spend more time in pondering than we do, if we better control our environments and desire to commune more often with our Father in Heaven.

Elder Joseph B. Wirthlin taught us some of the things we should ponder:

Parents should ponder over their family home evenings and their responsibility to teach the gospel to their family. All members should ponder over the instructions received in sacrament and priesthood meetings, in Relief Society, and in messages from home teachers. Priesthood bearers should ponder over their responsibility to honor their priesthood, to be examples of righteousness. Quorum leaders should ponder over their responsibilities to serve, teach, and strengthen their quorum members and to lead in love and kindness. Young people should ponder over problems that might confront them and be prepared to cope with them in a way that their parents, their leaders and their Heavenly Father would have them cope that they might keep themselves clean and pure. (*Ensign*, May 1982, p. 25.)

12

Acting or Reacting

A man was driving his car through a busy city intersection when the car came to a grinding stop and wouldn't move another inch. He got out, pulled a rifle out of the backseat, and pumped six bullets into the car engine. He was then arrested for shooting a firearm in a public place.

A young woman was dropped by her boyfriend, who started dating another girl, so she slashed the tires and convertible top on his new sports car to show how she felt. She was arrested and fined for her behavior, and yet did the same thing again.

A man was turned down for a job in an employment agency. As he walked down the street, he passed a bakery where they sold pies. After buying the biggest cream pie they had, he went back to the employment office and threw it into the face of the clerk who had refused to hire him.

Of a more serious nature are the following incidents: A man barricaded himself into a family's apartment and ended up killing three people because the man of the apartment had parked in his parking space. A teenager killed his friend with a knife because he wouldn't let him listen to his tape on the car stereo. A boy got a gun from his father's bedroom and shot his brother for changing the TV station against his will.

A person doesn't need a degree in psychology to realize that these people are not happy. Part of their unhappiness stems from the fact that they are not free. Many people allow themselves to be controlled by circumstances instead of taking control of their own lives and feelings. God does not desire us to be helpless and miserable. Lehi said:

Adam fell that men might be; and men are, that they might have joy.

And the Messiah cometh in the fulness of time, that he may redeem the children of men from the fall. And because that they are redeemed from the fall they have become *free forever, knowing good from evil; to act for themselves and not to be acted upon,* save it be by the punishment of the law at the great and last day, according to the commandments which God hath given.

Wherefore, men are *free* according to the flesh; and all things are given them which are expedient unto man. And they are *free to choose liberty and eternal life,* through the great Mediator of all men, or *to choose captivity and death,* according to the captivity and power of the devil; for he seeketh that all men might be miserable like unto himself. (2 Nephi 2:25–27, italics added.)

According to Lehi, we are free to act for ourselves, but sometimes we react instead of act. We allow people or circumstances to decide how we will feel and what we will say or do. If we meet someone who is angry, we become angry. If someone yells at us, we yell back. We allow others to be the control center for our own feelings and even actions by reacting to them instead of acting for ourselves. Sometimes others exert pressure on us, and as we react to the pressure, we do things that we know are wrong.

Rick, a sophomore in high school, was excited that he had made the football team. He wanted to join the lettermen's club but had to go through an initiation first. He was required to wear a white shirt, black bow tie, cut-off Levi's, and carry an eighteen-inch paddle and shoe-shine kit. He was required to do anything a member of the lettermen's club asked him to do or receive five hard hits with the paddle from each letter-man.

One day, a group of lettermen cornered Rick in the hall. They pointed to one of the assistant custodians who was men-tally handicapped and told Rick that they wanted him to fill his mouth with water and spit into the face of the custodian.

Rick lived in the same ward with the custodian and saw him every week at church. He refused to do it because it would be very offensive to both him and the custodian. There were five lettermen present, and they told him that they would give him five swats each if he didn't do it. He refused again and said that he would take the twenty-five swats rather than spit water in the custodian's face. Up to this point in the story, Rick is acting for himself and making good decisions.

Rick expected the paddles to hurt but not as much as they did. After two or three swats, Rick felt that he could not take it any longer and said that he would do what they wanted. With the boys watching, he filled his mouth with water and approached the custodian from behind. Rick tapped him on the shoulder, and when he turned around, Rick spit the water into his face and ran down the hall with the custodian chasing him and the older boys hooting and hollering.

Rick was free to act for himself, but reacted instead, and didn't do what he really wanted to do. He had other options, such as not joining the club, or taking a licking, or refusing to do something that would humiliate another human being, but he chose the one option that brought the most unhappiness to him.

After feeling guilty for several months, he finally ap-proached the custodian and apologized to him. Years later Rick became the bishop of his ward. As he was sitting on the stand, he looked at the congregation and saw the custodian sitting there looking at him. Rick was so grateful that he had apologized to him, but wondered what the custodian was thinking. He was still filled with regret for what he had done years before.

It is difficult to imagine a God that has poor self-control—one that reacts to situations instead of acting for himself. It's obvious that self-control is an important ingredient of celestial growth. When we remember that we are of divine lineage and are here upon the earth for a purpose, we tend to act instead of react.

Brad lived in a small farming community, and his property had been flooded out several times by irrigation water which had been carelessly left on until it had run onto his property. Since he wasn't a farmer himself, the water was more like irritation water than irrigation water.

One day he arrived home to find water pouring into his yard, and hustled down to the corner where he sent the water back down the main irrigation ditch. Just as he finished turning the water into the main ditch, the farmer who had flooded out Brad's property several times arrived at the corner and wondered what the "blankety-blank" he was doing. This farmer proceeded to call Brad every possible derogatory name he could think of.

Brad could have reacted and used some names that he was familiar with, but he decided to act for himself. When the farmer stopped to catch his breath, Brad kindly said, "I'm sorry you feel that way about me; I have always liked and admired you from the time I first met you."

The farmer was stopped completely in the middle of his tirade and was still fumbling for something to say as Brad climbed into his car and headed back to his house. The farmer later apologized, and from then on the two always greeted each other as friends. There is no doubt that self-control plays a major role in determining whether or not we are truly free.

There are at least five things that we need in order to be spiritually, physically, and emotionally free. The first one is *knowledge*. The more knowledge we have, the more good choices we can make. Since every commandment has a reward attached, the more commandments we can understand and keep, the happier we can be. Knowledge can open up new choices in every area of our lives.

I am not free at the present time to repair my car when it breaks down. When I was in high school I took a course in auto-mechanics, but my teacher was allergic to grease, so we were not allowed to work in the shop. We only read about repairing cars from a book. Because my knowledge is lacking in this area, I am not free to choose whether to fix the car myself or have someone else fix it. When I have car problems, I don't even bother to raise the hood, which action, by the way, is pushing my knowledge of cars some as it is. I do, however, have the choice of learning more about cars, which would then make me more free in this area.

Another thing that needs to be part of our existence in order for us to be free is *opposition*. Without opposition there is no choice. We can't decide whether or not to forgive someone if we are never offended. We would have no choice to make concerning smoking if there were no cigarettes. Without having the option of choosing evil, we could only choose the good, which would amount to having no choice at all. Without opposition there are no options and therefore there is no agency or choice.

A third thing that we need in order to be truly free is the *ability to choose*. Some are born into this world without the mental capacity to make important choices about right and wrong and, therefore, are dependent upon others. It appears from the scriptures that these individuals are heirs of the celestial kingdom.

Opportunity to choose is another thing that leads to total freedom. In many countries throughout the world this opportunity to choose is restricted.

Making correct choices is the fifth fundamental ingredient of freedom. This is not only one of the most important elements of freedom but also the one that is probably most overlooked and least understood. Most of us have the necessary knowledge, opposition, ability, and opportunity to be free. What we may overlook is the importance of making correct choices.

In the Gospel of John we read:

> Then said Jesus to those Jews which believed on him, If ye continue in my word, then are ye my disciples indeed;
>
> And ye shall know the truth, and the truth shall make you free.
>
> They answered him, We be Abraham's seed, and were never in bondage to any man: How sayest thou, Ye shall be made free?
>
> Jesus answered them, Verily, verily, I say unto you, Whosoever committeth sin is the servant of sin. (John 8:31-34.)

The more correct choices we make, the more choices we have available to us. Incorrect choices lead to fewer choices and less freedom than we had before. The amount of freedom we have either increases or decreases based on the kind of choices we make. Keeping or breaking the Word of Wisdom is an easy example to follow and illustrates this principle well.

If we decide to smoke, we restrict our freedom to make choices in so many ways. Physically, we restrict our performance in almost any activity we participate in. Studies indicate that a majority of adults who smoke want to quit but feel they cannot. They have lost the freedom to decide whether or not they want to smoke. Disobedience, however, nearly always affects us spiritually more than in any other way. Once we decide to smoke and thus disobey the Word of Wisdom, we lose the opportunity to receive the full promptings of the Holy Ghost. We restrict our opportunities to participate in the ordinances of the temple. We cannot advance in the priesthood, and we limit the callings in the Church that will come to us. We even significantly limit our opportunity to counsel our children wisely and encourage them to live the Word of Wisdom. Most of all, we limit the choices we will have for all eternity by making a choice that will prevent us from entering the celestial kingdom.

When we decide to live the Word of Wisdom, we open up

all of these other choices and still do not limit our freedom in any way. We can still smoke if we want to—we have just decided that we don't want to. At times we hear people complain about how restrictive or demanding the Church is. In actuality it is exactly the opposite. Through helping us understand the gospel and make correct choices, the Church helps its members become more free than any other people on the face of the earth.

At the beginning of the chapter, we discussed the importance of self-control. As we learn to act instead of react, not only do we take a giant step toward freedom, but also we become more like God and Christ. While Jesus was here upon the earth he set a perfect example of acting rather than reacting. He said and did what was right under all circumstances and conditions.

An interesting set of questions once appeared in a seminary lesson outline. Some of these questions are listed below and can help us evaluate how well we are controlling our physical actions and appetites:

1. Can you make your body smile?
2. Can you make your body laugh?
3. Can you make your body exercise properly?
4. Can you make your body memorize?
5. Can you make your body get out of bed early in the morning?
6. Can you make your body go without food and drink for at least two meals?
7. Can you make your body leave drugs alone?
8. Can you make your body kneel and pray?
9. Can you keep your body from reacting to evil thoughts?
10. Can you make your body resist temptation to feel anger, greed, hate, jealousy, envy, and pride?
11. Can you make your body enjoy reading the scriptures daily?
12. Can you make your body respond positively to promptings of the Holy Ghost?

Because God loves us and wants us to be happy, he allows us to choose for ourselves. He does not try to force or coerce us into making correct choices in the name of love. In fact, a war was fought in heaven to maintain our right to choose for ourselves. The reason for this is that love, kindness, mercy, forgiveness, and all of the other celestial traits that we are here to develop can only grow in a climate of love and freedom of choice. Because of this, we need to make sure that we allow those around us the climate they need to grow in. Elder Marion D. Hanks observed:

In matters of conscience and faith, if we truly love we will never seek to impose our will and deprive others of their agency. That is, after all, Satan's way. . . .

It is my deep conviction that any act or program or rule planned or performed without love at its heart, love as the spirit of it, or which curtails the agency of our Heavenly Father's children, is not worthy of God's kingdom or of his leaders or people.

Repeatedly He has protected our eternal agency, thus helping us to qualify through opposition and in the face of alternatives for the sweet blessing of eternal creative service. But we must choose—and be held accountable. (*Ensign*, November 1983, pp. 22–23.)

As we learn to control ourselves and act instead of react, we not only bless our lives but also the lives of others.

Yupha was a member of the *Woman's Welfare Services Society of Thailand*, and had been summoned to help at the scene of a terrible train wreck. As she arrived on the scene she was filled with revulsion and horror at the carnage that lay in front of her. As she wavered she heard a quiet voice say, "You are a Latter-day Saint. You must let your light shine for the world to see. You must be strong enough, patient, and brave enough to go and help."

Yupha took a deep breath and started pulling dead and injured bodies from the wreck. Suddenly she was attacked by a woman waving a stick who yelled at her, "My children are dead because of you! Look at the destruction your carelessness and negligence have caused!"

At first Yupha was confused by the accusations, but then realized that the woman had mistaken her for a railroad employee. She was calmly trying to explain that she was there to help when three police officers noticed the conflict and came over to help her. They warned the woman that they would arrest her if she harmed Yupha.

Instead of reacting in anger or fear, Yupha tried to understand the woman who had lost two children—one dead and one missing—and who was overwhelmed with grief. She turned to the policemen and said, "No, please don't harm her. She is only reacting out of grief."

When the police protested that she might be hurt, Yupha replied, "I'm not afraid. Heavenly Father teaches that we are all brothers and sisters; we must love one another. She will not harm me."

Yupha went back to work, and the police released the woman. Several hours later, after much heart-rending work, a call went through the workers for someone with type "O" blood. A small girl was about to undergo surgery and the hospital had exhausted its blood supply. Yupha volunteered and was taken immediately to the hospital, where she gave more than a pint of blood.

Not knowing that she should rest, she immediately went back to the wreck and continued helping others who were in need. Hours later, as she was preparing to return to her own family, a railroad official requested that all of the volunteer workers go to the hospital where the director wished to meet them and thank them personally.

The Minister of Public Health was also there and expressed his gratitude. While he was talking, the grief-stricken mother entered the room with one of the doctors. The doctor called out wanting to know if there was a Mrs. Yupha present. When Yupha indicated she was there, the woman ran to her and embraced her as she burst into tears. As Yupha stood there bewildered, the doctor said, "Your donation of blood saved this woman's daughter. She has come to thank you."

The woman said, "How can you stay so calm? When I have been so angry with you, you remain serene. What makes you like that?"

Yupha answered, "My church teaches that we are all brothers and sisters and should love one another no matter who it is or what they do."

Dr. Martin, the Minister of Public Health, was listening and was greatly impressed with Yupha and her answer. He had previously been head of the Department of Education, which was over the department that had imposed visa restrictions on the LDS missionaries. As he watched and listened to Yupha, he recognized the fruits of LDS missionary work.

The grateful mother requested more information about the Church and asked if she could come to church after the funeral had been held for her child. (See Carole Osborne Cole, *Ensign*, January 1981, pp. 56–57.)

We will never know how many lives have been or will be affected for the better because of Yupha and the strength she had developed to act for herself and not be acted upon. We can know with certainty, however, that our own families and others will be greatly blessed as we expand our freedom through listening to the Spirit and making the choices that lead to lasting happiness for all of us.

13

Nourishing Ourselves Spiritually

All of us are aware of the need to nourish ourselves physically, but we sometimes overlook our spiritual hunger and the kind of food that we need to satisfy it. Spiritual hunger is like physical hunger in many ways. Some of the symptoms of not satisfying both types of hunger are the same, such as weakness, irritability, and impatience.

Spiritual hunger is the deep spiritual need that we all have for Heavenly Father and his gospel. Many times we do not recognize this need until we are faced with an experience that awakens it within us. This experience may be some sort of crisis or disaster, or it may be the quiet prompting of the Holy Ghost as we are faced with an important decision or responsibility in our lives.

There are many positive signs of spiritual hunger. The desires we have to get closer to Heavenly Father, to learn more about his gospel, and to share the gospel with others are all positive indications of the inborn hunger for spiritual things that all of us bring to this world. Depression, a wavering testimony, contention, irritation at others, and a difficult time resisting temptation are negative signs of spiritual hunger or need.

One mother, after her seventh child was born, found herself feeling lonely, miserable, and constantly irritated by her other children. It took her seven months before she finally realized what the cause of these feelings was. Because of illness during her pregnancy, she had changed her routine of getting up early each morning to study and pray. She was still praying, but not with the same depth of feeling with which she had prayed after she had read the scriptures or general conference addresses for an hour.

She had felt justified in skipping her scripture study because she really was sick, but she had gradually become spiritually sick without even being aware of it. After several weeks of early morning study she felt strong and able to care for her family again. (See Molly H. Sorenson, *Ensign*, April 1977, p. 33.)

The reason this mother felt stronger and more capable was because she had discovered one of the best foods to satisfy spiritual hunger. Elder Boyd K. Packer discussed the kind of food needed to nourish ourselves spiritually:

In the mountains surrounding this valley there is still very deep snow. The animals, especially the deer, have suffered because of it. They have moved from the foothills to the orchards and gardens trying to find enough nourishment to survive. . . .

For many years game wardens brought alfalfa hay and established feed yards in the foothills. The deer came in great numbers to eat the green, leafy hay. They thought they were doing all they needed to do for them. But if the winter wore on and spring was late, the deer died in great numbers. They died of starvation with their bellies full of hay. This because nutrients essential to sustain life through a long period of stress were missing from their diet.

It can be like that with the flocks for whom we are the shepherds. Other stake presidents have thought they were doing all that was needed for their sheep, only to find that some have been fed but not nourished. Like the deer with their stomachs full of hay, in times of prolonged individual stress they do not survive spiritually. . . .

The right things, those with true spiritual nourishment, are centered in the scriptures. (Address delivered at meeting of Regional Representatives and stake presidents, 2 April 1982, Salt Lake City.)

In our quest for celestial growth amidst the concerns and distractions of a telestial world, it is easy to overlook or underrate the importance of nourishing our spirits through scripture study. Listed below are just some of the blessings that prophets have promised us if we make scripture study an important part of our lives:

1. Greater faith and spirituality
2. An increased desire to do the right, and increased strength to resist temptation
3. Inspiration
4. Increased knowledge, wisdom, and understanding
5. Answers to our problems and questions
6. Peace to our hearts and healing for our souls
7. Increased love
8. Greater satisfaction and happiness
9. Correction, instruction, and knowledge of the snares of the devil
10. Blessings in the home, such as less contention, increased love and consideration for others, submissive children, and peace, joy, and happiness

Examples could be given to illustrate that each of the above promises are fulfilled through scripture study. The following example has been chosen, however, because it illustrates the fulfillment of one of the most important and heartwarming, yet least understood, of all of the promises—the promise that scripture study can help heal "the wounded soul" (see Jacob 2:8).

A young man named Richard had rebelled against the teachings of his family and the Church. Many nights he would come home drunk, stand at his parent's bedroom door, and laugh at their concern. After his father had tried everything else, he said, "Richard, when you hit rock bottom, turn to the scriptures."

After he graduated from high school, Richard entered the military. He associated even more with friends that pulled him down, and he became heavily involved in drugs. He sank lower and lower until he became so depressed that he was committed to a mental hospital and confined to a padded cell.

After he had been in this condition for many days, he remembered his father's words concerning the scriptures and asked for a copy of the Book of Mormon. He didn't want to read the scriptures to improve his life, but rather to prove that his father was wrong. Richard was sure that there was no way reading the Book of Mormon could help him with his massive problems.

As he read through the Book of Mormon the first time, he marked over one hundred passages that he didn't believe in. He had nothing else to do, and in spite of his negative attitude something began to happen to him, so he decided to read it again, and again. Richard read the Book of Mormon seven times, and sometime during his reading he received a personal testimony that the Book of Mormon was true.

As his testimony grew, so did his desire and strength to put his shattered life back together again. Richard eventually knelt across the altar in a holy temple of God and was sealed to a wonderful daughter of God for eternity. (From James M. Paramore, in the *Hold to the Rod* series, Scripture Motivation lesson outline, lesson 4, p. 9.)

Now, the above example is fairly dramatic; we should realize that blessings that come from scripture study usually come gradually and quietly. Several individuals who had been studying the scriptures for less than a year were asked if they had noticed much difference in their lives because of their study. All twenty-one of them indicated specific blessings that they had received. They said such things as the following: I get along better with my family; my bad habits are easier to control; I have found real happiness as I have come to know God; coupled with prayer it is the most important thing I have ever done; I now know that God loves me; I have received the strength to live the gospel. There is overwhelming evidence that blessings really do come to those who sincerely read and study the scriptures on a regular basis.

A careful perusal of the scriptures shows that the Lord has never asked us to just read the scriptures; rather, he has asked us to study, seek, or diligently search them (see D&C 1:37; Jacob 7:23; Mosiah 1:7; 3 Nephi 23:1). Some people do not come to understand the scriptures or to receive the blessings promised therein because they skim through them instead of searching them. The process of diligently searching is portrayed very well in the following account.

A frightening, and yet ultimately inspiring, event will be remembered for quite some time among many residents of Utah. In the fall of 1989 a ten-year-old boy named Joshua was lost in an abandoned mine. He had gone into the mine with his father, a group of Scouts, and several leaders. Somehow he got separated from the group and eventually ended up in a six-foot-wide, twenty-five-foot-deep ore cavity. He had no food or water, and no warm clothing, matches, or flashlight. It was five days before he was found, and during that time he sang songs such as "I Am a Child of God," and prayed that someone would find him.

A search involving hundreds of people took place, with special rescue teams and trained dogs searching the numerous mine shafts. Sixty-five hundred man hours were spent in the search, and the mine was searched six times before the searchers were ready to call it quits and seal up the mine.

When a high priest named John heard that they were going to seal up the mine, he had a feeling that he needed to go back up to the mine and try to help one more time. His grandfather had been the mine superintendent and John had explored the abandoned shafts since he was eight years old. He had tried to help several times previously but had been told only trained experts could go into the mine, and he had been directed to leave the area.

Meanwhile, two other Church members, Brother Guymon and Brother Christianson, had been praying for some new leads. After four days of searching they knew they would need the help of the Lord in order to find Joshua. As Brother Guymon offered a fervent prayer in his motel room that night, he received a strong impression that he should search in a particular section of the mine again.

The next day, these three Church members looked over the maps of the old mine tunnels and began to search the area that Brother Guymon had been impressed with. They realized that this would probably be the last chance to find Joshua before the mine entrance was sealed. Around two o'clock in the afternoon, Brother Guymon heard a faint noise. He said that "it was a teeny, tiny noise like a little squeak." Even though he had heard a thousand noises during the past five days, it seemed as if the Spirit were telling him this noise was important. Brother Guymon had often been kidded about his poor hearing, yet he feels that the Lord helped him in this instance. The three men became completely still and heard a faint call for help. They eventually found Joshua huddled in the back of a small ore cavity, hidden from view by a load of debris. After five long days, Joshua had been found.

This story illustrates well the difference between searching and just looking. These people were committed to finding Joshua no matter how long they needed to search. They also realized the importance of having the help of the Lord and responding to his Spirit.

Too often in our scripture study many of us browse or quickly read the scriptures. We find our minds meandering from one concern to another and sometimes put very little mental or spiritual effort into our study. If we would search the scriptures with the same intensity and perseverance with which Joshua's rescuers searched for him, the scriptures would come alive to us and satisfy our spiritual hunger.

Many of us concentrate on getting through a certain block of scripture, like a chapter a day, instead of taking our time to search the scriptures for greater meaning and application. Several verses, searched carefully and understood, are much more beneficial to us than several pages or chapters read quickly. More searching seems to take place when we decide to search for so many minutes a day rather than read a certain number of pages or chapters. A time goal exerts no pressure on us to move quickly through the scriptures, so our time can be spent, if desired, looking up footnotes and studying more in-depth.

Of course it is always more helpful to have an idea of what we are searching for when we study. What we search for may depend on our spiritual needs. We may be looking for solutions to problems, insights that will help us better teach a lesson, guidance to help us in our family or Church responsibilities, or answers to specific questions. We can always be searching for concepts that we can apply in our lives that will help us know how to live better and how to draw closer to God.

Just as those that found Joshua followed the prompting of the Holy Ghost, we need the Holy Ghost in order to understand and apply the scriptures. The Savior said, "These words are not of men nor of man, but of me; wherefore, you shall testify they are of me and not of man; for it is my voice which speaketh them unto you; for they are given by my Spirit unto you, and by my power you can read them one to another; and save it were by my power you could not have them; wherefore, you can testify that you have heard my voice, and know my words" (D&C 18:34–36).

This scripture teaches us that it is through the power of the Spirit that we can come to understand the scriptures. It also teaches us that the scriptures are the voice and words of

Christ. Elder S. Dilworth Young captured the message of this scripture in a poem entitled "Know That I Am!" An excerpt follows.

Youth Speaks:

I do not seek thee, Lord
In highest hill or
Valley low.
The cloudy sky
Or stars which light the night
Are not thy face
I know.
Thou art the Son of God.
I thirst to touch thy garment hem,
To hear thy voice,
And to rejoice in thy
Calm presence, Lord.
A growing youth, I seek
To know thee and to
Hear thy word.

The Lord whom ye seek speaks:

My will is in my word:
Written in the rock
With iron pen,
Or graven in the
Gold of ancient plates.
My will is spoken
Unto men
Through prophets.
My voice speaks through
These chosen ones
Who write my words
On the page for all to see.
And reading them—
Given by my power

In the hour
Of their need—
They are my voice
To you,
Young friend,
And reading, you can say
That you have heard my voice
This very day.
(*Improvement Era*, April 1969, p. 49.)

Since the ability to understand the scriptures comes to us through the Holy Ghost, it is essential that we become receptive to the Spirit. We can become more receptive to the Holy Ghost as we do the following things:

1. *Desire to have the Spirit so we can better understand what the Lord wants us to do.* We need to be careful not to rely too heavily on the knowledge of others or our own intellectual abilities. We also need to maintain open minds and hearts, so that the scriptures continue to teach and inspire us and the Spirit can continue to guide our lives.

2. *Live the gospel better, which in turn moves us closer to the Lord and helps us better hear what he is trying to tell us.* An understanding of the gospel comes line upon line. When we live what we understand now, the Spirit will help us find more truth.

3. *Find a quiet place to study*—one where we can concentrate and have a minimum of distraction.

4. *Make pondering a part of our study.* Our study of the scriptures can, in a way, last all day if we allow ourselves time to ponder and contemplate what we have read. This means that the radio and TV could be turned off while we do the dishes or other chores so our minds are free to communicate with our feelings and with the Holy Ghost.

5. *Make prayer a regular part of scripture study.* Before studying we can pray for the help of the Holy Ghost, or we

can pray after studying for the strength and understanding to apply what we have learned.

6. *Spend a sufficient amount of time, put forth a concentrated effort, and study on a regular basis.* The more effort we make to understand and live the scriptures, the more the Lord will bless us with his Spirit.

7. *Read the scriptures themselves.* Listening to dramatized tapes and reading books about the scriptures will not bring the same blessings as studying the actual scriptures. They may be difficult to understand at first, but with the help of the Spirit we will soon become comfortable with the scriptures and will start to receive blessings that we cannot receive from any other source. The scriptures really are the word of God, and are the spiritual nourishment that we need in order to live celestial lives in a telestial world.

14

Removing the Venom

Consider the damage a person does to himself and others when he has an unforgiving or vengeful heart. Harold S. Kushner has written:

The story is told of two shopkeepers who were bitter rivals. Their stores were across the street from each other, and they would spend each day sitting in the doorway, keeping track of each other's business. If one got a customer, he would smile in triumph at his rival. One night, an angel appeared to one of the shopkeepers in a dream and said, "God has sent me to teach you a lesson. He will give you anything you ask for, but I want you to know that, whatever you get, your competitor across the street will get twice as much. Would you be wealthy? You can be very wealthy, but he will be twice as rich. Do you want to live a long and healthy life? You can, but his life will be longer and healthier. You can be famous, have children you will be proud of, whatever you desire. But whatever you get, he will get twice as much." The man frowned, thought for a moment, and said, "All right, my request is: strike me blind in one eye." (*When Bad Things*

Happen to Good People [New York: Avon Books, 1981], p. 117.)

Although this story is somewhat humorous, it nevertheless suggests a great truth. It is impossible to seek revenge or to desire to harm another without hurting ourselves. Because God knows this, he has asked us to forgive others no matter how horrifying their offenses. Jesus taught: "My disciples, in days of old, sought occasion against one another and forgave not one another in their hearts; and for this evil they were afflicted and sorely chastened. Wherefore, I say unto you, that ye ought to forgive one another; for he that forgiveth not his brother his trespasses standeth condemned before the Lord; for there remaineth in him the greater sin. I, the Lord, will forgive whom I will forgive, but of you it is required to forgive all men." (D&C 64:8–10.)

There seem to be several reasons why the Lord wants us to forgive others. One reason is that all of us offend, and so all of us are dependent upon the Savior for our forgiveness; we cannot expect him to forgive us if we won't forgive others. The Savior taught this well in the parable of the ungrateful servant.

There was a king who decided to settle his outstanding debts. One of his servants owed him ten thousand talents—a huge debt. Since this servant could not repay his debt, the king commanded that he and his family and all of their possessions be sold.

The servant fell down at the feet of the king, begged him to be patient with him, and promised him that he would eventually pay off his debt. The king was moved with compassion and forgave his servant of this huge debt.

The same servant then went to a man who owed him a hundred pence (a very small amount), grabbed him by the throat, and demanded payment. When this man begged for patience, the ungrateful servant rejected him and threw him into prison.

When the king heard about the servant's unwillingness to forgive such a small debt when he had been forgiven of such a large one, he was amazed. The king said, "Shouldest not thou also have had compassion on thy fellowservant, even as I had pity on thee?" and threw the ungrateful servant into prison until he could pay all that he owed.

After giving this parable, Jesus said, "So likewise shall my heavenly Father do also unto you, if ye from your hearts forgive not every one his brother their trespasses." (See Matthew 18:23–35.)

Another possible reason that God wants us to forgive is that it puts us in a position to help the offender. A few years ago a seminary teacher had a student named Phil that caused chaos in the classroom. Finally, in order to be fair to the rest of the students, the teacher had to ask Phil to check out of seminary. Although the teacher did this privately in his office, it soon became public as Phil, at the top of his voice, called the teacher several derogatory names. The students in the class could hear Phil very easily and were shocked when Phil threw open the door and ran into the room. He grabbed his notebook and Bible and proceeded to rip them up and throw the pieces of paper around the room. Phil then stormed out the front door and headed for the high school.

The first impulse of the teacher was to feel offended by Phil and desire never to see him again, but as he pondered the gospel principles of love and forgiveness, he decided to try to show Phil that he loved him. The teacher needed to go to the high school each day to pick up any information that the seminary needed, so he decided to make this trip during the lunch period each day in order to come in contact with Phil.

The first few weeks of contact were extremely difficult, but the teacher never gave up. At first, as Phil and his friends would see the teacher coming down the hall they would call him rude names and make fun of him. Each day in return the teacher would smile and say pleasantly, "Hi, Phil."

After two or three weeks, the name-calling got old, and when the teacher waved to Phil and said hi, Phil and his friends would just ignore him. After several months of this treatment, a minor miracle took place. Phil didn't call the teacher any names, and he didn't completely ignore him.

When the teacher waved at him, Phil actually raised his hand, just an inch or two, and gave a slight nod with his head.

It wasn't long after this that Phil was smiling and returning the teacher's greeting. They finally discussed the situation, and Phil came to realize that the teacher sincerely cared for him and had just been trying to do what was best for everyone concerned.

Three or four years later, the teacher was asked to teach a stake temple seminar for over one hundred couples who had committed to prepare themselves to be married in the temple. These were couples who had married out of the temple but who now wanted to become active and do what the Lord wanted.

When the teacher stood up in front of the group and prepared to teach the first lesson, who did he see sitting on the second row but Phil and his wife. As the teacher felt the promptings of the Spirit, he realized that Phil would not be sitting there if he had not paid the price of rebuilding their relationship during Phil's senior year in high school. The teacher would not have been in a position to teach or help Phil draw closer to his Heavenly Father.

A further reason for forgiving others is the effect it can have on our families.

In the early 1900s, a family joined the Church in Hawaii. They enjoyed their membership very much and were preparing to be sealed for eternity in the temple when one of their daughters became ill with an unknown disease and was taken to a hospital. The people among whom they lived were wary of such diseases because they had caused much death in the past.

The family went to church the next Sunday seeking the strength they knew they would receive from the members in their small branch. The father and his son were administering the sacrament, and had broken the bread and were preparing to kneel and offer the sacrament prayer. Suddenly the branch president realized who was at the sacrament table and called for them to stop. He told them that they could not handle the bread. "Your daughter has an unknown disease. Leave immediately while someone else fixes new sacrament bread. We can't have you here. Go."

The stunned father slowly stood up and led his embarrassed family out of the chapel. As they walked along the dusty trail back to their home, the son noticed his father's clenched fists and the set of his jaw. When they entered the room, the father had the family sit in a circle and asked them to remain silent until he was ready to speak.

The young boy thought his father was thinking up ways of getting revenge, such as killing the branch president's pigs or burning his house or joining another church.

After twenty-five minutes of silence, the family noticed a relaxing of the father's hands and heard a quiet sob come from his lips. Tears then started to trickle down his cheeks, and soon every member of the family was crying.

The father then opened his eyes, cleared his throat, and told his family he was ready to speak. He first turned to his wife and told her that he loved her. He told each child individually that he loved them. He then said, "I love all of you and I want us to be together, forever, as a family. And the only way that can be is for all of us to be good members of The Church of Jesus Christ of Latter-day Saints and be sealed by his holy priesthood in the temple. This is not the branch president's church. It is the Church of Jesus Christ. We will not let any man or any amount of hurt or embarrassment or pride keep us from being together forever. Next Sunday we will go back to church. We will stay by ourselves until our daughter's sickness is known, but we will go back."

Eventually the daughter was healed, and the family went to the temple. The children grew up and were sealed to their own families in the temple. Today over one hundred members of this family are active in the Church because the father was willing to forgive and apply this great principle in his home. (See John H. Groberg, *Ensign*, May 1980, p. 49.)

Still another reason for forgiving offenses and not seeking revenge is probably the most important reason of all: the Lord loves us and wants us to be happy. Nevertheless, some cannot understand why the Lord wants us to forgive those who have not expressed sorrow and are still offensive. Bishop H. Burke Peterson told a story that illustrates why God wants us to forgive everyone.

Some years ago, a group of teenagers went into the desert on an all-day picnic. They were playing when one of the girls was bitten by a rattlesnake. Venom was released almost immediately into her bloodstream.

This was the moment of critical decision. They could begin to extract the poison or they could search for and try to destroy the rattlesnake. They decided to avenge their friend by killing the rattlesnake, but it took them about twenty minutes to find and kill it.

As they returned to their friend, they became aware of her great discomfort and quickly rushed her to the hospital. By this time, however, the venom had had time to penetrate deep into the tissues of her foot and leg, and her leg had to be amputated below the knee. The senseless price of revenge had extracted its toll.

Bishop Peterson observed: ''There are those today who have been bitten—or offended, if you will—by others. What can be done? What will you do when hurt by another? The safe way, the sure way, the right way is to look inward and immediately start the cleansing process. The wise and the happy person removes first the impurities from within. The longer the poison of resentment and unforgiveness stays in a body, the greater and longer lasting is its destructive effect. . . . The poison of revenge, or of unforgiving thoughts or attitudes, unless removed, will destroy the soul in which it is harbored.'' (*Ensign*, November 1983, p. 59.)

God wants us to be happy, so he asks us to forgive others no matter what they have done. He realizes that we are not happy when our hearts are filled with hate and revenge. As we develop the strength to forgive others, we develop one of the great traits that we need in order to grow spiritually and become like our Father in Heaven.

During World War II, terrible offenses were inflicted on mankind. When the war was over and the concentration camps opened, many of the prisoners were not just pitifully weak physically, but their hearts were filled with hate as well. A prisoner from Poland, however, was found so robust and healthy and peaceful that the liberators thought that he must have either been recently imprisoned or not have undergone the atrocities that so many prisoners and their families had suffered. To their surprise, they found that he had been a prisoner for over six years and had been forced to watch as his wife, two daughters, and three small boys had been lined up against a wall and slaughtered with a machine gun.

The Polish father was a living example of the power of love and forgiveness. George G. Ritchie reports the words of this man, reflecting on the brutal slaying of his family, as follows: "I had to decide right then whether to let myself hate the soldiers who had done this. It was an easy decision, really. I was a lawyer. In my practice I had seen too often what hate could do to people's minds and bodies. Hate had just killed the six people who mattered most to me in the world. I decided then that I would spend the rest of my life— whether it was a few days or many years—loving every person I came in contact with." (In George G. Ritchie with Elizabeth Sherrill, *Return from Tomorrow* [Old Tappan, New Jersey: Fleming H. Revell Co., 1978], pp. 115–16.)

Sometimes an offense can be so painful that we cannot forgive without the help of God. Chief Blue had just such an experience. While hunting with six other Indians, Chief Blue's son had been shot by a man who had always been jealous of the chief.

Chief Blue's son was carried back to his home but died within a few minutes. When Chief Blue arrived home, he found that the man who had done the shooting was out in his front yard visiting with members of the crowd that had gathered. He did not appear to be upset.

Chief Blue's heart filled with hatred, and he thought to himself, "If you don't take down your gun and kill that man who murdered your son, . . . you are a coward." He had been a Mormon for many years and knew that he should not seek revenge but realized that he could not get rid of the hate he was feeling without the Lord's help.

Chief Blue walked out into the woods and asked the Lord to take the hate and revenge out of his heart. After a few minutes he felt better and started back towards his house. As he approached the house, however, his heart was again filled with revenge, so he returned to his place of prayer and prayed again.

When he felt better he headed back towards his house again, and once more he was filled with hate. This time he told the Lord that, without his help, he would become a killer, and asked the Lord to take the revenge out of his heart and keep it out. When he arrived at his home the third time, his feelings of hate and revenge were gone for good. (See Marion G. Romney, *The Power of God unto Salvation*, Brigham Young University Speeches of the Year [Provo, 3 February 1960], pp. 6–7.)

God has not left us alone but has promised us that he will help us when we are faced with obstacles that seem overwhelming and even insurmountable. Paul taught, "There hath no temptation taken you but such as is common to man: but God is faithful, who will not suffer you to be tempted above that ye are able; but will with the temptation also make a way to escape, that ye may be able to bear it" (1 Corinthians 10:13).

All of us will probably be offended by another at some point in time, and some of these offenses may be extremely formidable and painful, but God will help us replace the pain and hate with peace and love if we will turn to him and realize that he only wants what is best for us. Sometimes it takes weeks and even months to completely purge the poison of hate and revenge from our souls, but with the Lord's help it can be done. We need to place our trust in God and let him deal with the offender in his own time and way. Our responsibility is to do what we can to help ourselves, our families, and even the offender draw closer to God so that we can have his Spirit and eventually be like him.

We will rarely be more like God than when we forgive a brother or sister of offenses against us. The world around us is preaching revenge, but the still small voice whispers forgiveness, love, and peace.

15

The Celestial Equation

According to the Church-produced film *Man's Search for Happiness*, God has given us two great gifts—time, and the freedom to choose. How we use the minutes, hours, and days that have been allotted to us determines our future position and joy in the eternities to come. The scriptures indicate that a day for the Lord is equivalent to one thousand years as we measure time (see Abraham 3:4). Measuring our activities here upon the earth by the Lord's time instead of our own sometimes helps us realize how important it is to use our time wisely and make decisions correctly.

A man or woman who lives to be seventy-five years old has only been on the earth for one hour and forty-seven minutes based on the Lord's time. A "two-year" mission only takes 2.85 minutes. It only takes a fraction of a second to do our home teaching or visit the temple or have home evening with our families.

When we think of how long we lived before we came here and how long we will live after we leave this earth, the small fraction of time that we spend here becomes much more important to us. Every day we draw closer to, or move further away from, God and the blessings of the celestial kingdom by the choices we make.

In 1985 a study was made of what Americans eat, buy, and do during an average day. Some of the findings were quite humorous, but many were very sobering. For instance, each day Americans spend $700 million on recreation and entertainment; buy 50,000 new TV sets; smoke more than 86 million packs of cigarettes; produce 1.5 billion pounds of hazardous waste; toss 70 million quarters into arcade game machines; drink the equivalent of 28 million six-packs of beer; watch 1.5 billion hours of television; take 30 million sleeping pills; hand over $40 million to prostitutes; and drop out of high school at the rate of 14,000 students per day. (See *Deseret News*, 4 July 1985.)

Paul was describing the last days when he said that men would be "lovers of pleasures more than lovers of God" (2 Timothy 3:4). If we are not careful, we can become part of that prophecy. In modern revelation, after describing some of the events that would take place in the last days, the Savior said: "Hearken ye to these words. Behold, I am Jesus Christ, the Savior of the world. Treasure these things up in your hearts, and let the solemnities of eternity rest upon your minds. Be sober. Keep all my commandments. Even so. Amen." (D&C 43:34–35.)

Jesus does not seem to be suggesting that we should not enjoy life or have a sense of humor, but there is an important difference between being lighthearted and light-minded. It is important to think about why we are here and what we are trying to accomplish. When we remember why we are here, we use our time more effectively and make much better choices.

Although simply wasting time can be detrimental to our celestial growth, using time to fill our minds with garbage that passes for entertainment is even more dangerous. Most of us have heard of the garbage in, garbage out equation. In a lecture given to seminary teachers, Latter-day Saint musician Lex de Azevedo coined two other equations, which read:

$$TS = TT = TB = TK$$

Telestial Stimuli = Telestial Thoughts
Telestial Thoughts = Telestial Behavior
Telestial Behavior = Telestial Kingdom

$$CS = CT = CB = CK$$

Celestial Stimuli = Celestial Thoughts
Celestial Thoughts = Celestial Behavior
Celestial Behavior = Celestial Kingdom

There is no doubt that thoughts lead to behavior. Several studies have been done that indicate that when we experience an event vividly in our imagination it is recorded as actually happening. The part of us that develops habits and behavior cannot tell the difference between our actually doing something and vividly imagining it.

An Olympic skater who won a gold medal said that she would sit in her living room and skate through her program over and over again in her mind. She would hear the music and skate perfectly through every move. She even imagined herself receiving the gold medal each time she skated. She then said that when she actually went onto the floor she simply played back the tape in her mind.

Monitoring machines were hooked up to skiers while they were creating downhill runs in their minds. It was found that the muscles in their ankles received electrical impulses that matched exactly the twists and turns they would make while running the course. These impulses would continue until the skiers had actually finished running the course and come to a complete halt. Remember, they were only skiing in their minds. These skiers said that by creating their downhill runs in their minds they seemed to program muscles that then unconsciously made the right moves when they got out on the course.

The Lord said, "For as he thinketh in his heart, so is he" (Proverbs 23:7). Since we will eventually become what we feed our minds and spirits, it is important to restrict the flow of mental pollution and increase the flow of wholesome stimuli.

In counseling young men of the Aaronic Priesthood, President Benson discussed the importance of avoiding the trash often found in books, magazines, and movies: "We counsel you, young men, not to pollute your minds with such degrading matter, for the mind through which this filth passes is never the same afterwards. Don't see R-rated movies or vulgar videos or participate in any entertainment that is immoral, suggestive, or pornographic." (*Ensign*, May 1986, p. 45.)

To help his students understand the importance of avoiding mind pollutants, one teacher brought the ingredients for a fresh tossed-salad to class. He broke up the lettuce and added tomatoes and cucumbers while talking about how good the salad was going to taste.

The teacher then pulled out of a paper bag a package of Italian dressing and some vinegar in a bottle, and proceeded to mix them together. He then explained to the class that the key to a good dressing was fresh oil. He said he had tried several brands and had finally found the best oil for the job. Reaching into the paper bag again, he pulled out a quart of 10-40 weight motor oil. He explained that he used 10-40 in the summer and a little heavier weight in the winter, and then proceeded to mix the motor oil with the rest of the salad-dressing ingredients.

By this time, several class members were murmuring and becoming concerned that he was going to ruin a beautiful salad by adding motor oil to it. In spite of their objections, he told them that he was sure the oil would make it better, and poured the Italian, vinegar, and motor oil dressing over the fresh tossed-salad. Several groans issued from the class members as they saw and even smelled the motor oil as it mixed with the fresh vegetables and ran down the sides of the glass salad bowl.

The teacher then asked the class how much motor oil it would take to ruin their salad: a cupful, a spoonful, or just a drop or two. The consensus was that one or two drops would do the job. The class then decided that spiritual contamination was much more serious than eating a little motor oil.

As we allow inappropriate words and images to filter through our subconscious minds, we program ourselves to act in certain ways. The good news is that we can fill our minds with celestial material which will program us to think celestial thoughts and perform celestial acts.

Elder Packer told a kind of parable about a vacant corner lot to illustrate the importance of filling our minds with uplifting thoughts and ideas. This corner lot had a footpath and a bicycle path across it, and had become a collecting place for all kinds of junk. This lot did not become a junkyard all at once. It started with a few lawn clippings and some tree branches. Papers and plastic bags were added, and eventually old cans and bottles were dumped there. Even though no one had planned on it becoming a junkyard, little by little it had happened. Elder Packer observed:

This corner lot is like, so very much like, the minds of many of us. We leave our minds vacant and empty and open to trespass by anyone. Whatever is dumped there we keep.

We would not consciously permit anyone to dump junk into our minds, not old cans and bottles. But after lawn clippings and papers, the other things just don't seem all that much worse. . . .

Years ago I put up some signs in my mind. They are very clearly printed and simply read: "No trespassing." "No dumping allowed." On occasions it has been necessary to show them very plainly to others.

I do not want anything coming into my mind that does not have some useful purpose or some value that makes it worth keeping. I have enough trouble keeping the weeds down that sprout there on their own without permitting someone else to clutter my mind with things that do not edify. . . .

I've had to evict some thoughts a hundred times before they would stay out. I have never been successful until I have put something edifying in their place. (*New Era*, August 1979, p. 37.)

Within easy access to all of us are numerous reservoirs of knowledge and inspiration that we can fill our minds from. We can gain knowledge and understanding through the study of the scriptures and the many other uplifting books that are available to us. Apostles, prophets, and other Church leaders speak to us often, and their words are available in the Church magazines. We can gain strength and increased faith as we attend our meetings and mingle with other Saints. As we fill our hours with service to others, we will fill our own minds and hearts with greater love, empathy, and happiness. Church positions give us opportunities to serve that bring great blessings to us and others. Time spent with our families can be uplifting, enjoyable, and very rewarding. There are many TV programs that can teach and inspire us if we learn to be selective in our choices of entertainment.

We have only to look at the mission program of the Church to see the benefits of filling our minds with uplifting and worthwhile thoughts. Young men and women fill their lives with celestial food for eighteen months or two years and come home spiritually and mentally prepared to serve God and others for the rest of their lives. The discipline and spirituality that missionaries usually develop during their missions are invaluable.

Since the world will continue to offer us more and more spiritual pollution, we will have to work harder at filling our minds with spiritually nutritious food. Referring to the negative influences that seem to surround us in this world of the latter days, Elder Dean L. Larsen said:

In this difficult environment we will be expected to steer our own course in an upward direction. As President Kimball has warned us, it will neither be acceptable nor safe to remain on the plateaus where our present conduct has kept us. Abrupt downward forces, represented by increasing wickedness in the world, can only be offset by forces that move correspondingly upward. Our lives must be better than they have ever been before. This simply means that we will become increasingly different from those around us whose lives follow the world's way. It is not easy to be different. There are intense pressures that work against us. But we must clearly understand that it is not safe to move in the same direction the world is moving, even though we remain slightly behind the pace they set. Such a course will eventually lead us to the same problems and heartaches. It will not permit us to perform the work the Lord has chosen us to do. It would disqualify us from his blessing and his protecting care. (*Ensign*, May 1983, p. 34.)

There is so much good to choose from in the world that, with the help of the Holy Ghost, we can fill our lives with things of beauty and great worth. As we do, we will become what we came here to become—celestial people—and our lives will be filled with joy and purpose.

Personal
Revelation

Over one hundred people were asked how they decided what was right and what was wrong. The following ten answers are representative of most of the answers given.

1. By how I felt about it.
2. If I thought I would feel guilty, I wouldn't do it.
3. If I thought I would feel happy, I would do it.
4. I think of all the things that would happen if I did this or that; then I base my decision on that summary.
5. If everything turns out OK, then I know I made the right decision.
6. I don't know if it's right or wrong until I finish the task.
7. I think to myself, If I choose this will I regret not choosing the other?
8. I look at how it will affect me.
9. I try to think my decisions through to see what could happen.

10. You can usually tell if it is right by the results of your choice.

On the surface, many of these answers may seem reasonable and some of them even excellent, but with a little reflection, one can see that two important ingredients have been left out of the decision-making process in all these approaches.

Lehi and Nephi received a great vision representing this life and the things we need to do to partake of eternal life and the happiness and joy that our Father has prepared for us. In this vision, those who tasted the fruit of the tree of life were those who "did press forward through the mist of darkness, clinging to the rod of iron," that is, the word of God (1 Nephi 8:24). The idea of clinging to the word of God is an interesting one. Synonyms of the word *clinging* are *adhering, sticking,* and *bonding.*

Thus, the first ingredient for making good decisions is to consult the word of God. Since God knows so much more than we do, it would be foolish to make decisions without using his word for guidance and direction. Through his scriptures and leaders, he has given us his word on a wide range of topics, such as morality, abortion, honesty, family relationships, forgiving others, taking care of our yards, staying out of debt, handling disputes, and choosing proper forms of entertainment. The first step in making a good decision is to find out what the Lord has said on the subject.

The second important ingredient we need in order to make good decisions is to listen to the promptings of the Holy Ghost. The Holy Ghost can help us apply gospel principles to specific areas and situations in our lives. For example, we are commanded to help the poor and the needy and to share our temporal belongings. The problem is that none of us has enough money to help everyone; so how do we know whom to help and how much to give them? If we are in tune, and the desires of our hearts are right, the Holy Ghost will prompt us when the time is right.

One couple was sitting in a restaurant ordering their food when the waitress began to cry and had to go into the back room. When another waitress came over to take their order, the couple asked her what the problem was with the first waitress. With a little bit of prompting, she explained that the waitress was trying to raise her children alone and mentioned several negative things that had happened to her during the week. The final blow had come that morning when her trailer-home had caught on fire and most of her personal belongings and family necessities had been destroyed.

The first waitress finally got herself under control and finished waiting on the couple. As they chatted with her, they felt the Spirit soften their hearts and were prompted to help her financially. When they were through with their meal, they left a substantial amount of money on the table with a note telling her that they loved her and knew that the Lord loved her also.

The couple will never forget the feelings they received as they were getting into their car and glanced through the front window of the restaurant. The waitress had just picked up the money and was reading the note. She then looked through the window to see if the couple was still there. Tears of gratitude were running down her cheeks, and the couple suddenly realized that their gift was much more than a gift of money. Her face was a beautiful picture of her feelings, and they could see that her despair had been replaced with hope and that she no longer felt alone. As their eyes made contact with hers, tears welled in their eyes also and they felt a strong bond of love and fellowship. The Lord knew what the waitress needed and inspired this couple to help fulfill some of her needs.

Because people's needs are not always apparent, only the Holy Ghost can help us identify and fulfill them. A bishop discovered this truth early in his calling and would set aside one hour each week when he could be alone in his office. He would make sure that nothing was scheduled and would take the phone off the hook. He knew that his ward members had needs but had no idea what some of these needs were, so he would open the hour with prayer and spend the time thinking about the members of his ward. Many times he would take out the ward list and slowly read each member's name. On several occasions he was inspired to call people into his office and help them with problems. Sometimes he would begin by saying, "I don't know why I asked you here, but the Lord indicated that we needed to talk." Many times these people said that they had been trying to decide whether or not to call him and had been struggling with serious problems.

One of these people was a sister who had not been to church for as long as the bishop had been in the ward. When he asked her why she was not coming to church, she said that she didn't come because no one cared whether she was there or not. The bishop said that was not true and that he cared and the Lord cared. The woman began to cry and became a regular attender starting the next Sunday.

This weekly hour spent in communion with the Lord may have been the most productive time that the bishop ever spent because it put him in a position to receive guidance from the Holy Ghost.

Elder Boyd K. Packer said of the workings of the Spirit:

The Spirit does not get our attention by shouting or shaking us with a heavy hand. Rather it whispers. It caresses so gently that if we are preoccupied we may not feel it at all. . . .

Occasionally it will press just firmly enough for us to pay heed. But most of the time, if we do not heed the gentle feeling, the Spirit will withdraw and wait until we come seeking and listening and say in our manner and expression, like Samuel of ancient times, "Speak [Lord], for thy servant heareth." (1 Sam. 3:10.) (*Ensign*, January 1983, p. 53.)

Of course the Holy Ghost can do much more for us than help us make decisions and assist us in helping others. He can help us work out our problems and encourage us in times of trouble and distress. With his help, we can detect error and recognize truth, and the meaning of the scriptures can be revealed to us. The guilt we feel when we sin, prompting us to repent, and the beautiful joy and peace we receive when we are forgiven are great gifts that come from the Holy Ghost. He testifies to us that we are children of God and Jesus. The Holy Ghost gives us the power we need to fulfill our Church callings and to stand up for the things that are right. At times he even blesses us with the very words that we need to say.

The greatest gift that our Father gives us on this earth is the gift of the Holy Ghost. Elder Bruce R. McConkie said that the formula to receive personal revelation from the Holy Ghost is simple:

1. Search the scriptures.
2. Keep the commandments.
3. Ask in faith.

(*New Era*, June 1980, p. 50.)

The relationship between keeping the commandments and receiving personal revelation from the Holy Ghost is illustrated well in a story told by President Harold B. Lee.

President Lee was a stake president at the time and had spent most of the night directing a Church court which had led to the excommunication of a man. As he arrived at his office the next morning, he was confronted by the excommunicated man's brother, who told him that his brother was not guilty. When President Lee asked the man how he knew his brother wasn't guilty, he replied that he had prayed about it and the Lord had told him his brother was innocent.

President Lee invited him into his office and asked him a few personal questions. He found that the man was forty-seven years old and wasn't sure what priesthood he held, but thought he was a teacher in the Aaronic Priesthood. He didn't keep the Word of Wisdom, have family prayer, study the scriptures, or pay tithing, and he wasn't planning to pay tithing or to attend church as long as "that blankety-blank-blank man was the bishop of the ward."

President Lee then told this man about the radio that he had in his home. He said that when the radio was in good working condition, he could turn the dial to a certain station and receive the voice of a singer or speaker from great distances away. He went on to indicate that after much use the tubes inside the radio begin to wear out. When one tube wears out, static is received and the voices are not as clear as they were before. When another tube wears out, the voices on the radio may fade in and out and part of the message may be missed. President Lee then pointed out that eventually, if no attention is given to repairing the radio, it just sits there. Even though it looks like it did before, it no longer receives anything. President Lee's account of his interview with the man continues:

"Now," I said, "you and I have within our souls something that might be said to be a counterpart of those tubes. We have what we might call a 'Go-to-Sacrament-Meeting' tube, a 'Keep-the-Word-of-Wisdom' tube, a 'Pay-your-Tithing' tube, a 'Have-Your-Family-Prayers' tube, a 'Read-the-Scriptures' tube, and, as one of the most important that might be said to be the master tube of our whole soul, a 'Keep-Yourselves-Morally-Clean' tube. If one of these becomes worn-out by disuse or is not active—if we fail to keep the commandments of God—it has the same effect upon our spiritual selves that that same worn-out tube in the radio in my home has upon the reception we otherwise could receive from a distance.

"Now, then," I said, "fifteen of the best-living men in the stake prayed last night. They heard the evidence, and every man was united in saying that your brother was guilty. Now you who do none of these things, you say you prayed, and you got an opposite answer. How would you explain that?"

According to President Lee, the man then gave a classic answer. He said, "Well, President Lee, I think I must have gotten my answer from the wrong source." President Lee then went on to explain that we get our answers from the source that we list to obey. (*New Era*, March 1973, pp. 10–11.)

Sometimes we are not satisfied with our spiritual growth and feel that we are not receiving personal revelation from the Holy Ghost. Spiritual growth usually comes so slowly that we may not be aware of the help we are receiving from the Holy Ghost. Here is a list of attitudes that can help us better evaluate when we do or don't have the Spirit:

Have the Spirit

1. Desire to live the gospel
2. Want to be with others
3. Don't care if others see your actions
4. Feel peaceful and calm
5. Feel happy
6. Feel good about others
7. Good self-control in most areas of your life
8. Unselfish with your time Want to help others
9. Not offended very easily
10. Feel good about Church position
11. Desire to pray, and feel good about prayer

Don't Have the Spirit

1. Many commandments seem silly or restricting
2. Want to be alone and to be left alone
3. Are deceptive, sneak around, lie
4. Feel agitated and confused and angry
5. Feel unhappy and depressed
6. Feel critical or negative about others
7. Little self-control, easily angered or tempted
8. Feel resentful about demands on your time
9. Offended easily and often
10. Want other or no Church position
11. Don't want to pray in private or in public

Sometimes we desire some kind of miracle to take place in our lives so that we can develop instant spirituality or receive great revelations from the Holy Ghost. If we are not careful, we will forget Elder McConkie's simple formula of scripture study, obedience, and prayer, and go off in radical directions. For instance, one great man was not satisfied with the rate of his development and became a fanatic in his quest for spiritual growth. He flew to South America because there are higher mountains there. He felt that the higher he could get on a mountain, the closer he would be to God. To him, physical closeness had become confused with spiritual closeness. It is not surprising that his quest for special personal revelation actually led him further away from God and eventually ended in his excommunication from the Church.

Elder Packer stated:

I have learned that strong, impressive spiritual experiences do not come to us very frequently. And when they do, they are generally for our own edification, instruction, or correction. Unless we are called by proper authority to do so, they do not position us to counsel or to correct others. . . .

There is something else to learn. A testimony is not thrust upon you; a testimony grows. We become taller in testimony like we grow taller in physical stature; we hardly know it happens because it comes by growth.

It is not wise to wrestle with the revelations with such insistence as to demand immediate answers or blessings to your liking. You cannot force spiritual things. Such words as compel, coerce, constrain, pressure, demand, do not describe our privileges with the Spirit. You can no more force the Spirit to respond than you can force a bean to sprout, or an egg to hatch before it's time. You can create a climate to foster growth, nourish, and protect; but you cannot force or compel: you must await the growth.

Do not be impatient to gain great spiritual knowledge. Let it grow, help it grow, but do not force it or you will open the way to be misled. (Ensign, January 1983, p. 53.)

As we study the word of God, the Holy Ghost will prompt us as to what we should be doing and where we need to be improving our lives. This is the step of scripture study. There is peace and security in the guidelines that we receive from the scriptures and the leaders of the Church.

The second step is to apply what we learn. Not only will the Holy Ghost help us know what we need to do, he will give us the power to do it if we are sincere and pray in faith.

Praying in faith, of course, is the third step to greater spiritual revelation and celestial growth. Our prayers may include some of the following pleas: Please help me to understand the scriptures and apply them to my life as I read today. Help me be aware of those things that are most important for me to work on now, and give me the strength to change my life and live these things. I already know that I should be of service to others and should help build thy kingdom. Please help me today to be aware of the needs of others and guide me that I may do at least one thing today that will strengthen thy kingdom.

Like physical growth, spiritual growth comes slowly, but it can be accelerated by the desire of our hearts and the extent of our effort and service. There is a problem, however, with focusing in on spiritual growth as our primary goal: we can become self-centered and actually slow down the process of growth. Rather than focusing on personal growth, a better goal would be to strive to learn the word of God, serve others, and build His Kingdom. The Savior said, "He that loseth his life for my sake shall find it" (Matthew 10:39).

The missionaries that grow the most seem to be the ones who aren't thinking about themselves, but rather lose themselves in the service of God and others. The bishop that grows the most and receives the most revelation from the Holy Ghost is usually the one that is not dwelling on spiritual growth but is simply striving to obey the Lord and his leaders and to serve the people of the ward.

It seems somewhat selfish to desire to make adjustments in our lives simply so we can grow spiritually. A much better motivation for adjusting our lives would be our love of God and our desire to serve him, or our love of the people we have been called to serve and our desire to help them.

Thus we should put the Lord first in our lives and desire to serve him and others. Then our spiritual growth will happen automatically, and the help that we receive from the Holy Ghost will increase.

Index